SHINY SIDE UP

Road Dog Publications was formed in 2010 as an imprint dedicated to publishing the best in books on motorcycling and adventure travel. Visit us at www.roaddogpub.com.

Shiny Side Up; Musings on the Improbable Inclination to Travel on Two Wheels
Copyright © 2019 Ron Davis
All rights reserved.

Cover image by Tess Fitterling

ISBN 978-1-890623-72-2
Library of Congress Control Number: 2019945561

An Imprint of Lost Classics Book Company
This book also available in eBook format at online booksellers. ISBN 978-1-890623-73-9

SHINY SIDE UP

MUSINGS ON THE IMPROBABLE INCLINATION TO TRAVEL ON TWO WHEELS

by

Ron Davis

Publisher
Lake Wales, Florida

ABOUT THE AUTHOR

Ron Davis has been a rider, on and off, for about fifty years. Over that period, he's also squeezed in a full time career teaching high school and university classes in writing, photography, and publishing while also working as a social media writer for the tourism industry in Northwest Ontario and as an associate editor and columnist for *BMW Owners News*. In addition, his writing has been featured by *BMW Motorcycle Magazine, Volume One, Our Wisconsin*, and the National Writing Project, and his essays (some about riding) can be heard regularly on Wisconsin Public Radio's "Wisconsin Life."

CONTENTS

SHINY SIDE UP

1

How to Change Your Oil

Why pay those uppity mechanics to do something you can easily screw up yourself?

Satisfaction. Pride. Accomplishment. What can possibly compare with the feelings that surround doing a bit of motorcycle maintenance yourself? Well, probably nothing, except maybe the desperate feelings of anxiety over whether you've done something wrong that will leave you stranded on some desolate stretch of highway . . . at night . . . with no bars on your cell phone . . . in a downpour . . . but, other than that, wouldn't you like to know how to change your own oil? Yes, of course you would.

Let's get started. First, you're going to need some tools. A hammer, of course, is essential. Everyone knows you always need a hammer; in fact, I've heard that the original title of Pirsig's famous book was actually *Hammers and the Art of Motorcycle*

Maintenance. And those flimsy, cylinder cooling fins that get broken off so easily? They're basically just cosmetic anyway.

You'll also need a special BMW oil filter socket wrench attachment, part #GN-555-3398YK2-brgrdn~88Q59-nN-CIA007. Why do you always need some special tool to do anything on a Beemer? I imagine there are conversations going on all the time at BMW Research and Development that sound something like this:

"Hey, Hans, how are they going to get this dinky, little bolt off if they, say, have to replace this little light thingy in the blinker deal?"

"Oh, Helmut, they can use any kind of vise grips or pliers, maybe with a hammer; that'll work just fine, yah."

"*Ach Du Lieber*, Hans, did you forget we need more overtime this week? Let's make it so they will need this U-shaped, titanium, powder-coated, blind Torx-head driver I've just drawn!"

"Ummmm, could we make it metric, Helmut?"

"Of course, Hans!"

"Oh Helmut, You Rock!" (German equivalent of high-five)

You can get this nifty tool from a dealer, or you can spend a week on eBay and save yourself at least two or three dollars (before shipping, anyway). Or if you're the gambling type, just use your trusty hammer to drive a screwdriver into the side of the filter. Then you can either simply crank out the filter or, that failing, trailer your bike to your nearest dealer and try making up a story about how the bottom half of your oil filter got torn off. (Like, they won't already know.)

In addition, you'll need something to catch the oil drained from your bike. Now, you can spend your hard-earned money on a specially designed, galvanized steel drain pan, or you can take the more thrifty route like I did and purchase one of those foil, turkey roasting pans, which will work just fine, at least until you actually need to use it, in which case you'll find the way you bent it up to fit in your side case has resulted in pinhole leaks you won't notice until the hot oil starts spreading over your garage floor. But rest assured, you can feel good about the fact you have saved another five, maybe six, bucks.

To remove your drain plug (to use the technical term) you'll need something called an Allen wrench, a tool taking its name from the famous German toolmaker, Reinhard Wrench. If you can't remember where you put yours after you used it trying to unplug that pesky garage floor drain, you can always substitute a big screwdriver, vise grips, and of course, the hammer.

Warning: don't start hammering on your bike until you've also picked up some oil and a new oil filter. Don't get me started on what kind of oil to use; recent research shows that ninety-five percent of all BMW rally altercations involving fists and specialized BMW tools have begun with seemingly innocent conversations about oil. Really, you can get oil anywhere, just make sure the label says something about "visigosity," has a seal from the United States Bureau of Standards and Measurements (USBOSM), and above all, make sure it has an anabolic-transfat rating of at least 39.5 millibars. If not, you're in for big, big trouble. You'll need at least two extra quarts, since obviously one will get knocked over and the other will be placed in your side case for emergencies, but will be lost after you remove it one day to make room for bananas, milk, bread, and olive loaf.

Now you're pretty much ready to begin the process:

Step 1: Run the bike until warm, but consider that just running it in your closed garage may not get the oil circulating as freely as it should.

Step 2: Find hammer. (It's probably still out in the lawn where you hit it with your mower last week.)

Step 3: Remove drain plug. Oh yeah, when you pick up the oil filter, part #SN543-UV30-R1600-GARM-?-BRTWRST1, they're probably going to try to talk you into buying something called a "crush washer." This is a needless expense just dreamed up by corporate fat cats in the nuts, bolts, and washers cartels. If you give in and buy one, you'll find it's just going to get crushed, just like your old one.

Step 4: Slide turkey roasting pan under the hot oil stream now pouring onto the garage floor. (If you slide it under there before you begin, the drain plug will fall in there, and, you know, that oil can stay hot for a long time . . .)

Step 4.1: Frantically start pulling off reams of paper towels to form mini-booms around the spreading oil spill headed for your clogged garage floor drain.

Step 4.2: Begin cursing your yellow lab who, suddenly tired of licking your face, has decided to walk through the growing oil puddle on her way into the house.

Step 5: Grab nearest aquamarine towel to try wiping up paw prints on carpeting before wife gets home.

Step 6: Remove oil filter, burn self, drop filter, spilling contents on garage floor.

Step 7: Replace drain plug. You'll find that in a real service manual for your bike they will give you mysterious directions such as, "Tighten drain plug to 45Nm." The *Nm* is a meaningless abbreviation mythically referring to torque force, but in actuality it simply means, "one or two light taps with hammer."

Step 8: Remove oil filler cap and pour in one quart of oil.

Step 8.1: Grab more paper towels to clean up the new quart of oil on the floor, since you forgot to replace the oil filter.

Step 9: Replace oil filter after applying a thin coat of oil to the gasket (that rubber part). Note: If it hasn't happened already, this would be a good time to kick over an opened container of new oil, since it's going to happen at some point anyway.

Step 10: Continue pouring in oil until the oil reaches the proper level in something called the "sight glass." There are different schools of thought on exactly where the proper level is. You should probably spend the remainder of the day on one of those online forums to check the indicated levels for your latitude, longitude, elevation, distance from the sun, day of the week, moon phase, time of day, mental disposition, etc.

Step 11: Almost done! Take bike for a shakedown cruise. You'll notice I did not say "replace filler cap," since, if you're like me, you neglected to do that once on your F650 Funduro and had the hot oil spurt up all over your face shield and your new hi-vis yellow touring jacket, and from now on, well, that step obviously goes without saying.

Special Note: Upon returning your bike to the garage, make sure to park it out of all that oil spill you spilled, but don't worry about standing in it yourself. This will allow your feet to slip when you're putting the bike back up on it's centerstand, which will cause the bike to fall over on it's right side, which will necessitate calling your neighbor, Wally, over to help pick up the bike, which will prompt him to all the while make cruelly hurtful remarks about your prowess as a mechanic. On the upside, though, Wally will most assuredly throw his back out.

You did it! To sum up then, let's compare . . .

Oil Change at a Dealer	DIY
Parts, Lubricant: $35	Five Quarts Oil: $45
Labor: $30	Kitty Litter (for oil spill): $3.29
Tax: $3.50	Foil Turkey Roasting Pan: $3.29
Total: $68.50	Carpet Shampoo: $9.97
	Dog Shampoo: $3.79
	Paper Towels (1 case): $11.99
	Aquamarine Guest Towel: $10.50
	Oil Recycling Fee: $5
	Gas (for miscellnaous trips to town for paper towels, guest towel, shampoo, kitty litter, recycling, etc.): $20
	Wally's 12 Chiropractor Appointments: $360
	Total: $474.52

Your savings: Well, rather than thinking about savings, best to think about the intangible benefits of changing your oil yourself. The pride, the sense of accomplishment, the humility, the pain, the exasperation, the anger, the marital discord . . . well, just remember: YOU DID IT YOURSELF!

2

How to Lose Friends and Influence Absolutely No One

I feel sorry for those who will never be able to experience the joy of riding a motorcycle. Never will they be able to share in the heart-throbbing exhilaration of hitting a snow squall on a deserted stretch of highway, wet flakes frosting their face shields like wedding cakes. And speaking of face shields, never will cagers share in the spine-tingling excitement of watching a hornet crawl across the inside of their face shields while streaming down an interstate at eighty miles per hour. And speaking of interstates, never will drivers feel the invigorating blast of a straight-line wind driving them perilously close to guard rails. Yeah, not being a rider really sucks.

However, there are certain unfortunate consequences of being a motorcycle enthusiast, certain occupational hazards that have nothing to do with the physical aspects of flying down the highway. I'm talking about social consequences. Say you, the lifelong rider, are at a neighborhood cocktail party. Mingling over your rum and Coke, you decide to bring up some intriguing tidbits of information you picked up from recently reading a short history of Bing carburetors. Your audience blinks, searching for a connection to their ongoing discussion of in-ground sprinkler systems. You drift away to another cluster, and spotting Dino, the dinosaur in an antique Sinclair Oil sign above your host's basement bar, you launch into a summary of the various schools of thought on the origin of the BMW roundel. Your discourse is worthy of a freshman research paper (complete with citations), but . . . crickets. Somehow, knowing the name of Hans Muth's dog, or the incredible run of sixties-era BMW sidecar victories turns out to be, socially, the equivalent of having breath that smells like a bucket of walleye guts . . . after three days . . . in the sun.

And at the family dinner table? I'd recommend avoiding bringing up your opinions on trail braking and delayed apexes, at least unless you want your brood to pick up their plates and migrate into the living room to watch reruns of *Say Yes to the Dress*. Even in the car with your spouse, you may find she or he frantically cranks the radio's volume knob to hear the latest on pork belly futures when you try to point out an example of upside-down front forks. And the *coup de grace* liable to bring any social encounter to a panic stop is a red-faced tirade on cell phones that blames their use for everything from distracted driving to climate change.

This, then, is the moto-enthusiast's curse: forced to stifle our wealth of road stories and encyclopedic motorcycle knowledge and knuckle under to the social pressure to speak of children or pets, weather, and the latest cat video gone viral. But there is shelter from the storm: rallies, getaways and club gatherings. There you can mention, to approving nods, the classically elegant lines of the 1994 BMW R 100 R Mystic or commiserate over the inability to cancel a service prompt without your own GS911 or a service charge. And occasionally serendipity smiles on us when we randomly meet someone who shares a history with bikes. Just the other day I met a ninety-two-year-old who told me a story about the Harley he had in the forties: "It was just after WW II, needed new pistons for my Flathead. My dad took me to see a buddy who run a little machine shop on Water Street. After lookin' through a big, greasy parts book on the counter, the guy put down his cigar, said he figured he had some from a '39 Mercury V-8 that'd work. Turned out, the piston skirts were too long, so he cut 'em down and dug up some rings. They slid in like they was born there; compression just about doubled—Wow, did that baby go! Course I still got a scar down here on my leg from where the kickstarter snapped back . . . " Great story, much better than hearing how Precious, your neighbor's Lhapsa Apso, chased a chipmunk.

There's no doubt about it, we're outliers . . . or . . . is it possible we're the chosen few, those who have been transported, on two wheels, to the transcendent clarity of the promised land? Through eyes crusted with grit and insect parts, perhaps we are the ones who see through all the mindless, mundane minutia. Maybe they, the less fortunate, mock and shun us because it's easier than admitting that we ride the twisty road of enlightenment while they drive the soporific, soulless slab . . . That must be it! What a relief! Now, where did I set my rum and Coke?

3
BATHING IN THE ROAD

Just the other day I coasted up to a stop light at a busy city intersection, grabbed some brake, clutched, and put my left foot down . . . into a pool of fresh oil. I nearly went down, but as my foot slid, I caught just enough grip at the edge of the puddle to be able to shift my weight to the right side. I edged backwards frantically trying to smear off as much of the oil on my boot as possible before the light changed, and after pulling out, I obsessed over how slippery my boot remained, lightly skimming the pavement with my foot, trying to "deglaze" the sole.

As with most of these close calls, my first reaction was to get generally ticked off, but with a cooler head later on, I started to consider there might be a positive side to the constant dangers we riders are prone to. Potholes, tar snakes, sandy corners, wet leaves, road gators, plastic bags, branches, critters, glass, nails, distracted drivers—the list of potential pitfalls is endless. One night I even had to slalom through a pair of plastic tire chocks somebody had mindlessly left in the highway—that could have ended very badly. That cagers never have to worry about this stuff is one more aspect of motorcycling that makes it a singular experience, but I've begun to consider it's not necessarily a negative one.

As I think Pirsig once wrote (and I'm probably murdering his prose), when you're in a car, you're watching a movie; when you're riding a motorcycle, you're *in* the movie. And Tolstoy said something like, the "now" is the most important time, because it is the only time we have power. Other philosophers have said that though they might appear vitally pressing, the past and future are illusions, reality is in the moment. Riding a motorcycle is one of those activities that, like jumping out of an airplane, forces us to live in the moment, at least if we want to survive, and that could be part of why we choose to do it.

I was listening to an NPR story a couple weeks back that examined the idea of "Shinrin-yoku" or "Forest Bathing." Though the idea has been around probably forever, it's a practice that was recognized in the 1980s in Japan as an avenue to preventive health care and healing. As I understand it, forest bathing is a kind of guided therapy that encourages participants to sit down or walk by themselves in the woods to let stress and the nagging bugaboos of everyday life fall away, thereby reducing anxiety, depression, and anger. The objective is to slow down and immerse oneself in the sights, sounds, smells, and physical sensations of a pastoral moment. Apparently, this kind of structured, bucolic meditation is growing in popularity across America, and there is actual medical evidence that it lowers blood pressure, reduces levels of stress hormones, and enhances the activity of white blood cells known as natural "killer cells." People using the therapy say they find their forest bathing rejuvenating, like hitting a reset button. Well, Duh! Who doesn't enjoy a solitary walk in the woods?

What's this got to do with motorcycling? Well, maybe we are "road bathers." Obviously, miles on the road can't offer the same benefits as moments of quiet reflection in a forest, but consider riding a motorcycle as meditation. Every spring I have to rehearse the mental algorithm of stopping and starting successfully on a steep incline. Underway, my mind is jumping back and forth between visualizing my line in each curve, shifting smoothly, making a tight U-turn, planning an exit strategy at every intersection, and working the mantras of so many other second-by-second protocols. Add to all these ongoing operations the constant vigilance for danger, not to mention the almost overwhelming sensory input of flying down the highway, and where else could a rider be but "in the moment?"

Of course, for more than one reason, riding a motorcycle will never make much sense to many people. When my daughter asks if I can take her for a ride on my Beemer, her husband rolls his eyes in exasperation and shakes his head. Not wanting to breed marital discord, I tell her my F700 is a single-rider bike (it isn't). One of my best friends sends me links to news stories about horrible motorcycle accidents. My daughter-in-law, the nurse anesthetist, tells me transplant surgeons call the onset of motorcycle weather "harvest season." I can't deny a simple ride on a bike can go south at any moment, but neither can I say there are many other activities that rivet me so much into the moment . . . and make me feel so much more alive.

4

WHAT'S YOUR SIGN?

Much has been written about "The Wave." Do you wave? And just who do you wave to? However, this ongoing discussion only demonstrates the pitiful paucity of hand signals we as riders have in our communal toolbox. Is this the only unspoken communication we, those rendered mute by helmets, face shields, and growling motorbikes, can come up with? Obviously, we need a new, much more comprehensive vocabulary of hand signals, so I have humbly suggested some possibilities below. You're welcome.

1. I'm driving here! Lots of moto safety experts talk about "conspicuity,"

and there may be some evidence that it actually makes a difference, but I'm not sure any gesture, short of emulating Ratso Rizzo (Dustin Hoffman) in *Midnight Cowboy* and pounding on a driver's hood, will get every driver's attention. Would it be over the line to mount one of those white, school bus strobes on top of my helmet?

2. Seriously? You're going to pull out now? I guess this could be simply pointing a finger (your index finger) at any driver about to enter from a side street or driveway, whose zombie-like stare seems to be looking right through you. Frantically waving your left arm, flashing your lights could be enhancers, but I'm not guaranteeing it will make any difference. Finley  Peter Dunne said, "Trust everyone, but cut the cards." In our case, the second part should be, "but cover your brakes."

3. My butt is dead. Okay, I don't care what kind of fancy custom seat or seat covering you've got—gel, beads, air cushion, a virgin yak pelt—I can't believe there doesn't come a time when all riders have to stop and let their near-deceased derrieres get some relief. My suggested gesture to let your riding pals know of your distress could be pointing at your butt then gingerly patting it. Of course,  you could also get up on your pegs and suggestively waggle your rear end around, but let's face it, no one really wants to see that.

4. Warning: watch road for tire snakes, road gators, dead skunks, mattresses, water bottles, garbage bags, high heeled shoes, bungee cords, ice chests, muffler pieces, etc.! Pointing urgently at the pavement to warn riders seems pretty vague when you consider all the drek that we find strewn over the road, but at least it might get your companions to look down. Come to think of it, I  forgot to add "shovel" to my list. I once watched one of those bounce out of landscaping crew's trailer directly in front of me. Fortunately, it cartwheeled into the ditch and didn't decapitate me. I caught up with the crew at the next stop sign and told them what happened, and the driver actually had the nerve to ask me if I would run one of his guys back to get the shovel, since it would be so inconvenient for him to turn the rig around!

5. Back off! I have no suggestions for a gesture that politely conveys, "Please, kind sir or madam, GET THE &%# OFF MY BUTT!" without risking road rage (though I can easily think of four or five that certainly would!). Maybe just a single "hands-up" motion might express your apology for having the incredible audacity for using the same roadway with someone whose need for that extra five miles per hour I'm sure is a vital matter of national security, even if you're bound to catch up to him or her at the next light. There is no shame (but probably lots of wisdom) in pulling over at the first opportunity.

6. Were we all dropped on our heads as children? Smacking yourself in the forehead could probably convey this question to other riders who have cheerfully chosen

to join you on that trip to your "special burger joint" and experience the sublime wonder and delight of riding in rain, hail, wind, fog, and/ or 100 degree heat down the wrong turn-off when everyone else in the world is back on their couches munching popcorn and

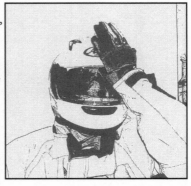

binge-watching *Game of Thrones*. It better be a good burger.

7. Speed trap ahead! I've heard there are gestures to let approaching riders and drivers know that they're headed

into the sights of Officer Friendly's radar gun. It could be circling one raised index finger to simulate a spinning cop light, but that seems a little anachronistic. How do you simulate a strobing LED? I've also heard tapping the top of your helmet is supposed to make oncoming motorists think of those Smokey the Bear hats troopers wear. Either way, you've first got to consider the ethical question: "Do I really want to warn them?" What if the oncoming driver is the same guy who was tailgating you yesterday?

8. Nice bike! Maybe a sweeping flourish with the left hand and a slight bow, as if you're saying, "After you." This gesture would obviously be reserved for BMWs—well, maybe for a Ducati, but only the Multistrada.

9. I'm begging you, please hang the &$#?@ up and drive! What good is it being a columnist if you can't rant

about issues your family has now forbidden you from bringing up again? I've become the consummate, crusty curmudgeon when it comes to drivers using cell phones. I mean, seriously, if they're in a parked car to begin with, why do they wait until they're entering traffic

to make a call? So far, all I've come up with is making that little finger and thumb "call me" gesture, but I have a feeling, as far as expressing the true fathomless depth of my loathing, we're having "a failure to communicate." They know they're on the phone. They know it's illegal. Who do I think I am, anyway?

10. Deer Ahead! No ethical dilemma here. Of course I want to alert all oncoming traffic to four-footed kamikazes lurking ahead; no way do I want to carry any more bad karma down the road than usual. Pointing to the side of the road, spreading the fingers of your left hand next to your head to simulate antlers, using the "stop" signal (palm up) to urge them to slow down—at the

very least, gestures like those make me feel better.

11. Nature calling. I can think of all kinds of hilarious gestures I could use that would convey my need to hit the head, none of them approved for family audiences. Much more tasteful: just point at your gas tank, as in "need to stop for gas." Might as well make it a two-fer.

There is a book out there by Baine Kamp, aptly titled *Motorcycle Sign Language*, not to mention a bunch of websites that attempt to catalogue and suggest ideas for hand signals, but unless there's universal acceptance, that's all they remain, just suggestions. I invite our faithful readers to add to my meager list of suggestions—as Joan Rivers used to say, "Can we talk?"

5

THE TIE THAT BINDS

One sweltering day last summer I was stopped at a red light when a pretty young lady in an SUV pulled up next to me. Her window was down, and looking my way, she leaned out and asked, "Aren't you hot?" A quick side note here: this was a question, emphasis on the word *hot*, probably prompted by my wearing an improbable three-season motorcycle jacket. Regrettably, this wasn't an exclamation, as in "Aren't YOU hot!" I smiled and said, "Yup, but as soon as I'm on the highway I'll be okay."

A few miles down that highway I had to pull into one of the ever-present convenience stores for gas and had another encounter there that I'd bet is familiar to any rider. As I was filling my tank, a guy from the next bay over walked up, grinned, and said, "Where ya headed?" What followed was a lengthy conversation about my bike, his BMW riding days, and the pleasures and perils of motorcycle life in general, ending with smiles all around and a hefty handshake.

These kinds of encounters have happened so often to me when I'm on a bike I practically expect them whenever I'm at the pump, a wayside, an overlook, a campsite, or yes, even at a stop light. And the probability of being accosted seems to go up exponentially according to the amount of gear (or road grime) I have layered on the bike. I like it. Everyone that approaches me seems to have a story or a question, and though I'm far from being an extrovert and not the kind of person who seeks out new relationships, these moments can turn a routine stop into an opportunity for a pleasant and often interesting chat with a complete stranger.

And apparently, I don't even have to be on the road. This morning a realtor stopped by to look at our house, and when we got to the garage, all talk of septic tanks, land values, and interest rates came to an immediate halt when he spied my Beemer. A DRZ400 rider himself, Patrick and I played twenty questions over the merits of BMWs versus Suzukis for the next ten minutes, and I guess now we're buddies.

Last June while on a solo trip, I bunked one night in a fishing cabin. The cabin was set back in the sticks, and I purposefully pulled in early in the evening, since I didn't want to try navigating gravel roads and deer crossings after dark. There was no TV, no wireless, no phone service, and I had eaten an early supper. I unpacked my stuff, and thought to myself, "Well, now what?" I set to cleaning up my face shield, when just then a woman with curly blonde hair opened the door and walked in, taking me by surprise. Startled herself, she said, "Oh, excuse me, I just came to get some ice; didn't know anyone was here!" We quickly introduced ourselves, and then she asked, "Is that your BMW out there?" When I told her it was, she continued, "Nice bike. Say, what are you doing tonight?"

I looked down at my bug-encrusted helmet and said, "Well, I guess this is it."

"Don't move," she said, holding up one finger, "I'll be right back!"

Now, I must admit, I had a lecherous moment there, wondering if this was code for the old cliché, "Let me slip into something comfortable," but ten minutes later, Lacy (the blonde) and her husband (John) came knocking, laden with a platter of three artisanal cheeses, locally smoked trout, crackers, a bottle of Pinot Grigio, and two six-packs of Two Hearted Ale. It seems that Lacy and John, although then "glamping" from a jeep carrying a couple kayaks and a mutt named Jordy, had been at one time cycle tourers, crisscrossing the country on John's beloved K 75.

While we sat at my cabin's picnic table and watched the West Fork of the Kickapoo gurgle by, we ate, drank, shared our knowledge of attractions in the area, and traded all kinds of stories. John, a "Coastie" who had worked security and rescue out of San Francisco Bay, shared an experience he had had while ferrying his K-bike back to Wisconsin. In Utah, a strong, straight-line wind suddenly slammed across the highway, and John watched the semi he was following tilt and then tip onto its side on a corner. At the same time, the blast drove him off the pavement, across the shoulder, and down into a ditch, where he and the bike did an endo. Luckily, Lacy had been following in the Jeep, and miraculously, the only fatalities were a crushed headlight nacelle and a fractured collar bone. Now that's a story! We adjourned to a campfire, and the story spinning and bonding continued long into that starry night.

The next morning, I was packed and squirming my way back to the highway by dawn without an opportunity to see my new friends again, but it occurred to me how lucky I had been—once again saved from the solitary confinement of my own noggin and probably a night spent reading a John Sandford novel for the third time, simply due to my choice of transportation. Much as I was fond of believing when I was sixteen, motorcycles are not chick magnets, nor are they only about spending time by yourself. They can be, however, a link, a password, or a secret handshake that often admits me unconditionally into a community of like-minded people. Like it or not, it's in our DNA to be social creatures, and it's strange (a little wonderful) how a hunk of steel and plastic can fulfil such a basic human need.

"Chopper 90"

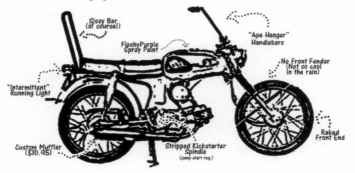

Sissy Bar
(of course!)

"Ape Hanger"
Handlebars

FlashyPurple
Spray Paint

No Front Fender
(Not so cool
in the rain)

"Intermittent"
Running Light

Raked
Front End

Custom Muffler
($10.95)

Stripped Kickstarter
Spindle
(jump start req.)

6

To Every Time
There Is a Motorcycle

My first bike was a 1965 Honda S90. Well, sort of an S90. You see, a buddy of mine, Kurt, had taken a standard (and severely abused) Honda and "reincarnated" it into kind of a hideous ode to the Big Daddy Roth School of Design. He had added a three-foot sissy bar, ape-hanger handle bars, and a bullet-shaped muffler, discarded the front fender, raked the front end, and spray painted the whole thing in a sparkling purple finish.

Kurt sold me the bike and an oily cardboard box of parts for fifty bucks, after his dad (a doctor who had seen his share of cycle mishaps and had caught Kurt riding without a license) gave him twenty-four hours to get the monstrosity off the property. I knew absolutely nothing about motorcycles, but it was the sixties, I was fifteen, and I thought the bike looked cool. I dreamed it would it would give me celebrity cred with girls and a new tier of respect from my friends, though they promptly dubbed the implausible-looking vehicle, somewhat derisively, the the "Chopper 90."

It had a number of idiosyncrasies, most notably a stripped kickstarter spindle, which meant that in order to start the bike, one had to run along, pushing the bike with the clutch in, hop on, drop the clutch on second gear, and bump start it. It, as a rule, never started on the first try, probably due to my forgetting to set the choke/open the fuel petcock/turn the key/put it in second gear/etc. The second attempt usually offered the best odds of bringing the little motor sputtering to life, since I was still hopeful and fairly fresh, but with the third and fourth, optimism, speed, and my ability to impress girls would steadily deteriorate. I'm sure there were times when I had run halfway to my destination before the bike fired up (or I gave up completely). When I did get the bike running, I remember I was very reluctant to park it any distance from a good hill, even if that meant stopping blocks away from my destination. Thinking back, the ten-block route to school really might mean me riding only three, but somehow that was still worth it.

On the other hand, once started, that Honda had the little engine that could. A tank of gas seemed to last forever, and at thirty-three cents a gallon, running it was practically free. The Dixie Cup-sized piston could rev to scary heights forever, and the crankcase never leaked a drop of oil. Granted, on hills the bike kept you busy downshifting while trying to sustain forward motion, and I also learned to allow lots of lead time before pulling out on a highway, but that Honda could pull you and your girlfriend just about anywhere, as long as you didn't care how long it took. We didn't.

Although Kurt the Customizer obviously had been big on cosmetic changes, he apparently wasn't too interested in details like the electrics. The tail light, for instance, shown brightly with the bike parked, but seemed to cut out as soon as the bike started to move, which along with a flickering headlight, could make the Honda virtually invisible from the back at night. The brake light worked, though, which, on the nightly rides home from my girlfriend's, often left me frantically tapping the brake pedal and redlining the engine in an attempt to escape the semi that always seemed to be bearing down on me.

A little about the girlfriend: she loved riding on the back of motorcycles (even the rolling joke I rode) but hated helmets (which at the time were legally required). She said something about freedom and the feeling of her hair blowing in the wind (it was, after all, the sixties). She also always wanted to go faster and had a way of persuading me, which, well, I can't really describe for a family audience. Fortunately, my top speed for the S90 hovered around forty-seven miles per hour. I should mention that same girlfriend lived at the end of a two-mile long sand road. In its original incarnation the Honda could have frolicked off-road, but as a pseudo chopper, it shimmied and squirmed so much through the sand that I had to slog the entire two miles with both legs out to prevent putting the metal side down.

Preposterous as it was, the S90 lasted through high school and a year of college, whereupon I finally decided to sell it and move up to something more respectable, a souped up red and white CB350, but that's another story. The guy that bought the 90 planned to restore it to its showroom state, and I hope he did, but I never saw it again. Many different bikes and adventures were to follow the "Chopper 90," but come to think of it, that bike had taught me some important lessons:

1.   OEM is not the enemy. Sissy bars may look cool, but catching your foot on one as you swing your leg over the saddle and falling over the bike (followed by the bike falling itself) doesn't.

2.   Use your trip counter. Back in 1965 there was no such thing as a fuel gauge on the tea cup piston-ed Hondas. Though the S90 got nearly ninety miles per gallon, eventually it would, of course, run out of gas. There's something imminently humbling about pushing a dead motorcycle down the highway as everyone you've ever known drives by.

3.   I will never be a mechanic. Despite my efforts to correct that stripped kickstarter spindle on the S90 (torqueing the clamp until it cracked, inserting homemade spacers,wire, attempting to drill into hardened steel), I was forever bound to bump starting.

4.   Carry a kickstand pad. Coming out to the parking lot after being imprisoned in a sweltering high school classroom all day, about the most discouraging sight I can think of is seeing your bike lying on its side, baking on the soft asphalt in a pool of leaking gasoline.

5.   Motorcycles do not necessarily impress girls. See items 1, 2, 3, and 4.

6.   Wear a helmet. My dad, bless his soul, would only begrudgingly allow me to ride my Honda if I wore the purple flake helmet Kurt had generously thrown in as part of the deal. A lowside while rounding a sandy corner made me consider my dad might not be quite as ignorant as I thought he was.

7.   Lights, kind of important. Especially on a dark, moonless night. In the rain.

8.   Mufflers can be hot. I had a buddy named Joe who had lots of mechanical experience. Under the tutelage of his stock car driving brother, he had even completely disassembled and reassembled the engine in his aged Buick Cutlass (though it only ran intermittently after that). When I rode over to his house to get some expert advice on the bike's numerous mechanical problems, my first move was to grab the muffler. I spent the rest of the day helplessly watching him tinker, my hand in a bowl of ice water.

9.   All mechanics are not created equal. When I reached the end of my patience with my kickstarter problem, I finally

bit the bullet and rode the bike out to the local Honda dealer. One of their mechanics (maybe a year older than myself) said, "Let's just weld it!" He then proceeded to lay the bike down on its side and dragged the arc welder over. As gas began to drip onto the garage floor, he flipped down his helmet and began to glob some brass onto the fitting. I casually back-walked twenty feet out the shop door, finally appreciating the wisdom of Shakespeare's "Discretion is the better part of valor." (The weld lasted a day.)

10. Girls trump everything. Sometimes the bike actually ran. And miraculously, my girlfriend loved to ride with me. Though the Honda still had its passenger strap, she would wrap her arms tightly around me and put her chin on my shoulder as we tooled along. Somehow, this made all the inconvenience, all the frustration with mechanical issues, and all the occasional mortification that the "Chopper 90" produced more than worth it.

Looking back, that Honda had done exactly what a good bike should do: it perfectly suited my bank account, skills, common sense (or lack of it), and lifestyle, all the while getting me to where I wanted to go as fast as I needed to, well, most of the time anyway . . .

7

A MEASURE OF A
MOTORCYCLIST

On March 24, 1999, Italian Pierlucio "Spadino" Tinazzi mounted his BMW K75 and headed out to his security job at the Mont Blanc Tunnel, the passage deep beneath the highest peaks of the Alps, which straddles the border between Italy and France. Part of Tinazzi's job was to patrol back and forth through the tunnel, coming to the aid of motorists and keeping traffic moving through the seven-and-a-half mile shaft.

The Mont Blanc Tunnel was an engineering marvel when it was finished in 1965 after four years of construction. By 1999 an estimated 5,000 cars, trucks, and motorcycles were passing through the tunnel daily, saving the motorists at least seven hours of driving time through mountain passes when transiting from southeastern to northern Europe.

Tinazzi had been drawn to motorcycles all his life and had even turned down a promotion that would have had him riding a desk in the control room instead of a bike, since he enjoyed riding so much. As he climbed the mountain to the tunnel entrance at about 4,500 feet above sea level, the sun shone brightly and a southern breeze, unusual for the area, carried the promise of spring. After making one of his morning runs, Pierlucio paused for a break just outside the French entrance.

At that moment, a white Volvo FH12 tractor trailer headed toward Italy was approaching the halfway point in the tunnel when the driver, Belgian Gilbert Degraves, noticed white smoke emerging from under the truck's cab. Degraves pulled over and jumped down to grab his fire extinguisher, but almost immediately, the underside of the truck burst into flames and smoke began filling the tunnel. Degraves began running for the Italian entrance to get assistance.

What had seemed initially like a simple engine problem within minutes became a raging inferno, belching thick black smoke flowing toward the northern entrance and engulfing trucks and cars stalled behind Degraves's semi. As the fire spread, exploding tires and gas tanks sent shrapnel ricocheting off the tunnel walls. Melting wires doused the tunnel lights, and the black, cyanide-laced smoke reduced visibility to zero.

Meanwhile, alarms at the French entrance began to sound. Pierlucio "Spadino" Tinazzi quickly grabbed his helmet and breathing equipment, started his BMW, and began the three mile trek toward the tunnel's center. As he encountered panicked drivers on foot, he directed them to stay low, take breaths near ventilation ducts, and use the tunnel sides to find their way out; others, too overcome to walk, he carried out on the back of his bike. Somehow threading his way through the smoke while dodging bodies and burning wreckage, Tinazzi made four trips in and out of the hellish scene, but on his fifth trip in he discovered an alive but unconscious truck driver he couldn't get onto his pillion seat. Tinazzi dragged the driver to "Niche #20," a small, pressurized refuge compartment with a fire door designed to protect those inside for two hours.

The Mont Blanc Tunnel Fire burned for over fifty hours, reaching temperatures estimated at over 1,200 degrees Fahrenheit, and is estimated to have been equivalent to a blaze created by five to seven flaming fuel tankers. As Tinazzi's BMW melted into the pavement, which itself had begun to burn, he and the driver perished. Of the fifty drivers and passengers who had found themselves trapped behind the burning tractor trailer, thirty-seven died within the first fifteen minutes (accounts of the number of deaths differ), but at least ten survivors emerged, all claiming they owed their lives to "the man on the motorcycle." While other first responders and fire fighters had tried to enter the tunnel, they were rebuffed by the fire and smoke, and none made more than one attempt. In fact, many had to be rescued themselves.

The day of the tragic Mont Blanc Tunnel Fire was full of sad ironies. Forensic investigators theorize that the fire in Degraves's truck had begun before he even entered the tunnel, probably caused by a cigarette tossed from an oncoming car and sucked into the air intake above his cab, where it ignited the air filter. (All vehicles now pass through a thermal scanner before entering the tunnel.) Subsequent simulations of the tragedy indicate the conflagration could have been avoided if Degraves had never stopped, since by pulling over, the fire suddenly got enough oxygen to erupt, igniting his fuel tanks and cargo. Also accelerating the fire was the uncharacteristic southern breeze and an Italian control room operator's decision to flood the southern half of the tunnel with fresh air to protect drivers he saw fleeing toward the southern entrance. The tunnel had effectively become a colossal chimney fire. The trucker's load of seven tons of margarine until then was considered to be a safe substance, but surrounded by the highly flammable polystyrene insulation of the refrigerator trailer, the cargo transformed into something akin to napalm. Also, though some of the drivers caught behind Degraves's Volvo nearest the entrance did attempt to reverse or make U-turns to escape, vehicles closest to the blaze wouldn't start because of the lack of oxygen.

What isn't ironic is the way Pierlucio Tinazzi's bravery has been honored. He was awarded posthumously the Medaglia d'Oro al Valore Civile, Italy's highest civilian honor for bravery, and a gold medal for heroism by Switzerland's Federation International de Motocyclisme. A plaque commemorating Tinazzi's heroic act was also installed at the Italian entrance to the Mont Blanc Tunnel. But the most impressive tribute is made every year by the hundreds of motorcyclists who travel to the Mont Blanc Tunnel on March 24 for the "Spadino Memorial." With the tunnel closed to all traffic except motorcycles, riders of all types swarm over both lanes to ride from one end of the tunnel to the other and back in a somber homage to Pierlucio Tinazzi's sacrifice.

Following the fateful day of the fire, France and Italy spent three years renovating the safety features of the tunnel. Instead of control rooms at each end of the tunnel, one central control room was constructed to avoid communication problems. Quarters were also built for a full-time fire crew in the middle of the tunnel, and new exits for escape to a ventilated passageway under the tunnel's surface were also installed, along with new, more protective safety compartments.

Like it or not, when you choose to ride a motorcycle, you automatically join a community that is often judged by the non-riding world on the basis of the behavior of its most notorious members, whether engendering respect or contempt. As members of that community, we should be proud to be associated in any way with the motorcyclist Pierlucio Tinazzi.

For more information about Pierlucio Tinazzi, I'd recommend reading "Backmarker: Searching For Spadino," a poignant account by Mark Gardiner, author of *Riding Man*. The article can be found at motorcycle-usa.com. For an excellent examination of the fire itself, search youtube. com for "Seconds From Disaster: Tunnel Inferno."

8

THE HAPPY CAMPER

As if riding a motorcycle wasn't challenging enough, some of us have chosen to camp from one. In that I have an extremely illustrious history of both motorcycling and camping (in other words, I have, so far, survived) I'd like to offer some sage suggestions on the subject of "moto-camping" which, in all truth, I'm pretty sure you could live without:

1. Take everything. I mean everything. Feel free to load every pound of what may seem like superfluous, self-indulgent luxuries. Battery-operated coffee grinder? Sure! Golf clubs? Why not? Boom box? Weed-wacker? Chainsaw? It really doesn't matter, since it's been my experience that by piling on every kind of accessory you can think of, you'll promptly throw your back out the first time you try lifting the laden bike up onto its centerstand and will have to cancel the trip anyway.

2.   It's not camping without a campfire. Campfires are in our DNA. There's nothing like satisfying that primitive urge to make fire by foraging for a bundle of firewood (five dollars for three pretty pieces of birch at the campground store), building an intricate teepee of tinder (road map, toilet paper, spare tent poles), and settling back to stare dreamily into the embers as your buddy trips over your tent ropes (breaking one of your tent poles) and steps into the fire. Though watching that same buddy (who's now made snarky remarks about your pitching your tent so close to the fire) burn his fingers on his travel mug left on the fire ring or getting sprayed by an exploding can of beans can be pretty rewarding, too. Since building a campfire always produces a sudden cloudburst forcing you inside, it's also wise (if not fairly hilarious) to pitch your tent upwind of the fire ring, so your buddy's tent is the one that fills with smoke.

3.   Showing the flag. When I was a "rally virgin" I arrived early and set up camp in a field sparsely populated with other tents and bikes. I had to chuckle as I watched my fellow members erect little flags from their tents or bike mirrors, thinking this was some silly rally tradition. I then spent my first MOA rally day going to workshops, wandering through the vendor area, and gawking at all the bikes, only to be eventually corralled into the beer garden, where I spent hours discovering the new-found camaraderie of my rider brethren and the pithy eloquence produced by dark beer. Wobbling back to my tent in the dark and surveying the endless sea of nearly identical tents that had sprung up while I was gone, it dawned on me that flying a flag might not be so silly.

4.   You will need a shovel. My dad liked to take me camping when I was kid, and he was obsessed with always digging a trench around the edges of our enormous, moldy canvas tent wherever we were. The idea was to ditch the perimeter of the tent to keep the rain (it always rained) from seeping under the tent. However, since we never seemed to dig a trench leading away from the tent, we usually awoke surrounded

by a mud-filled moat that eventually overflowed and made puddles in the tent floor deep enough to support aquatic life. Digging the trench (usually my job) was done with a green, WWII-issue folding shovel. I remember my father taking a thoughtful drag from a Lucky Strike and informing me that during the war shovels like ours were carefully sharpened by our troops to produce a darling weapon of last resort capable of dismembering any enemy within striking distance. Quite the lovely image to pass on just before bedtime to an imaginative eight-year-old who could now have nightmares of armless, headless Nazis roaming the campground. I don't carry one of those now; however, as I have an exceptional talent for selecting campsites next to groups who party until 3AM, singing along with endless renditions of Ted Nugent's *Back Scratch Fever*, I have often wished I did.

5.   Eat. Eating is important; in fact, many will say if they had to give up a physical activity, eating might at least be their second or third choice. And yes, you can choose to pack freeze-dried coq au vin, prune-infused trail mix, powdered beer, and other foods you would never consume anywhere else under any other conditions. But you can also choose to drive the five miles into town and search out Clyde's Coffee Cup (or Katie's Quick Lunch, the Crystal Café, etc.). The cook there, a guy affectionately known as "Chain," will have a ponytail and a Harley parked out back. He will come out to ask about your bike and tell you about a charming little stretch of twisties just outside town. And, oh yeah, a waitress named "Dottie" will call you "Hon." Again, your choice.

Don't get me wrong. I like to camp from a motorcycle. In fact, I'm fairly certain, even with my highly questionable memory, I can recall just about every spot I've ever pitched a tent, whether it turned out to be a delight or a disaster. Motel rooms, not so much.

9
LOOKING BOTH WAYS

3 seconds, 3 inches, and riding has never been quite the same . . .

It's January, and the bike is in the basement. As I stoke the woodburner and take a Saturday afternoon to attend to all those little maintenance chores I put off during the riding season, I flash back to three seconds last summer, the same three seconds that have, since then, entered my thoughts every time I've pulled on my helmet.

On another Saturday afternoon last July, I had decided to take a little jaunt into the city to pick up a few last minute items I needed for a fishing trip with my son. After finishing my shopping, I pulled on my hi-vis jacket, checked the modulating headlight, and began to thread my way through the mall parking lot. I rolled cautiously to the exit and came to a stop at the traffic light at the intersection with the busy frontage road. First in line, signaling left, I waited for my green arrow. My thoughts drifted to the logistics of next week's trip.

I got my arrow, looked both ways, and began to ease out into the intersection when suddenly to my left a silver SUV came careening through the intersection, blowing through the red light at around fifty. I grabbed, I stomped, I skidded, and the idiot's bumper flew by three inches from my leading Metzler. Feet down, I stood for a moment, wide-eyed and transfixed. All the other motorists' eyes at the intersection exchanged the same look. One woman, directly across the lane, squinted and shook her fist, trying to convey her sympathy with my shock and disbelief.

I felt dazed and shaky, but eased out the clutch and crawled across the intersection. It wasn't my first near miss, but after a few blocks I realized this wasn't just another close call. I needed to pull over into the nearest parking lot for a little decompression. A cup of coffee or two later, I set out again, but the blurry movie of the speeding SUV relentlessly looped through my thoughts all the way home.

Unique experience? Hardly. I'm sure anyone riding a bike, even casually, has their share of close encounter stories—the pickup pulling out of an alley, the minivan turning left across your lane, the semi roaring up behind you as you slow for road 'gators strewn across the interstate—but there was something different about this one.

Was it the utter disregard that driver had shown for the most basic of basic traffic rules? From what I had been able to glimpse, the driver wasn't on a cell, he was looking straight ahead. I mean, it was a red light, wasn't it? Don't we have a deal about this? Is it conceivable the driver deliberately ignored the light? Was it an emergency? There is no way of ever knowing, but every detail of the incident continues to haunt me.

Maybe that's a good thing. Experts like David Hough would probably say moments like that keep you sharp (and possibly alive). It's the "Trust everyone, but cut the cards" mindset that I think most seasoned riders inevitably adopt. I know hazards like the sandy corner and the deer standing in the ditch come with the territory, but after an incident like this, is there any rider who hasn't asked him or herself this question: Is this worth it? Can I enjoy the ride or do I want to ride with the creeping conviction that everyone's out to murder me?

I never told my wife about the fateful three inches (pretty sure she'd rather not hear about it), but as we stood hip deep in a trout river a few weeks later, I mentioned it to my son. Ever since the time I pulled into his driveway one March morning on an F650 after slogging through a snow squall, he just shakes his head whenever I bring up bikes, and he greeted this story with his usual skepticism, if not a little contempt.

"Did you tell Mom about this?"

"No, I didn't."

"I wouldn't." He stopped hauling in his line for a moment and turned to me. "What if you had gotten hit?"

"That would have been bad, I guess."

"Not just bad for you. You know what I mean?" I did.

Did the incident at the light steal some of my love for motorcycling? Yes. Will I stop riding? Not yet. Risk has probably always been part of the attraction. But along with some of my riding confidence, some of the joy for riding that SUV stole from me doesn't seem to be coming back.

I remind myself that it's only January. I tighten a few bolts, polish some more chrome, and wonder where the 1150R will lead me next summer. There's still enough joy there to keep me pulling on my helmet, stabbing my start button, and rolling on the throttle. But I'll always look both ways. Maybe twice.

10

THE EXTRACTION

After a long, cold winter on the "Frozen Tundra" here in Wisconsin, we usually can expect to be teased by a day or two of unseasonably warm weather in March. However, I've fallen for that false promise of spring before and vigorously fight the urge to bring the bike out of dry dock before April Fool's Day. Though, come to think of it, holding off probably has less to do with my strength of will and more to do with the effort it takes to get my bike back on the road. You see, I'm one of those guys who actually brings his bike into the house for four or five months.

I do have a garage, but it's a small one, only one stall, and it's unheated, so I know I would worry all winter long about the effects of pogo-ing temperatures. As my favorite BMW mechanic once told me, "These bikes don't like to sit in the cold." Adding to my worry would be a possible smooch from my snowblower or my wife's Ford, not to mention my garage's open door policy when it comes to mice.

But I also have more selfish reasons for bringing the bike in. There's a special kind of comfort that comes from being able to sneak a longing look at the bike every time I go down to the basement to stoke our wood burner. After all, a bike left in the garage can get lonely. And, on a sub-zero weekend, being able to fondle and farkle in a cozy space with close proximity to a comfy rocking chair and a "beer fridge" (a Wisconsin tradition) is hard to beat.

So my bike waits on its centerstand mid-November through March, but once our road has slipped the bonds of its icy slicks and ruts in April, preparations for the extraction begin. First, I call up my buddy, Ralph, for some help. He invariably gives me his usual, "You know, I'm a pretty busy guy" (he's been retired for four years) and then agrees to drive over. Ralph owes me, since some years I've also stabled his Bonny in my basement space. Next, I start prepping the runway. The threshold to our basement is raised about ten inches, so ramps have to be set up, the basement door has to be removed, and laundry baskets, miscellaneous drum set parts, bins of Christmas ornaments, and my wife's monstrous elliptical machine have to be repositioned. On the bike, mirrors must be folded in, bar ends slipped off, and luggage racks removed.

Once Ralph arrives, inevitably, a little dance has to take place before the actual bull work can begin. There's a bit of stalling while Ralph recites his usual collection of wiseacre remarks, knowing he has me in his power: "Doesn't your daughter have a big, strong boyfriend?" and "Isn't that my torque wrench?" and "I see your exercise machine makes a nifty clothes rack." Then we do a little review of how this is going to work—Yes, Ralph, once more, you will push, I will ride. A diabolical progression of close quarter Y-turns gets the bike headed the right way, interspersed with various grunts, groans, unintelligible directions, and Ralph's hilarious mock exclamations, brought to a standstill, of course, by the UPS guy showing up with a package from Amazon.

Getting through the door is the hard part. My handle bars measure thirty-four inches, the doorway is thirty-two, so there's considerable leaning, twisting, frantic commanding, and a clinched-teeth interpretation of the terms *left* and *right*. Finally the bike and I coast down the other side and out into the first sunlight the bike has seen in five months.

The big finale is seeing if the motor will actually start. Invariably, the kill switch has gotten nudged, the key hasn't been turned, or I've forgotten the kickstand has to be up, but in most cases, like a melodramatic TV defibrillator scene (Clear!), the bike comes to life. The grip is twisted, the throaty exhaust clears its throat, and it's suddenly bike season again.

But the ritual is not over. Ralph collects his well-earned payment of a cup of coffee and a morning bun from our local Trout Bum Bakery, but he senses I'm eager to go for a ride so gathers his little white dog Jack and cuts his visit short.

Taking the bike out on the road is a tentative, cobweb clearing affair, full of the familiar, first-ride-of-the-year fumbling. My shifts are tentative, I toddle through the turns, and I realize reviving last year's skills and confidence will take some miles. However, in April, the roads feel endless and my bike's return to its winter home in my basement seems decades away.

11

WE ARE WHAT WE SPEAK

A VERY BRIEF GUIDE TO MOTORCYCLING TERMINOLOGY

I broke my leg when I was twenty-four. Actually, I should say Boscoe, my best friend's dog, broke my leg. He had a habit of launching himself at full speed and piling into unsuspecting bystanders like a furry, seventy pound cannon ball. He licked my face as I writhed around on the ground, and it slowly occurred to me I would not be starting my new job in two days (trimming Christmas trees) or moving my stuff to my new place that weekend. Boscoe, in a matter of seconds, had reduced me to 155 pounds of dead weight, which luckily, my older sister would feed and shelter for the next two months.

After the R&R and on two reasonably sturdy legs again, I was desperate for an income and took the first job I could find: piling lumber on the night shift at a local sawmill. Looking back thirty years, I'm amazed at my resilience. To go from languishing on a couch to throwing fresh-cut, red oak railroad ties around in the dark on ten-degree January nights makes me wonder who I was then. I lasted there three or four months and would be hard-pressed to remember many of the details of that job (though, come to think of it, there weren't all that many), but I do remember one morning. I had gotten home at the usual 4AM and, too exhausted to go to sleep, I began writing a note to my girlfriend about my job. Somehow the letter evolved into simply a list of the words that had become part of my new sawmill vocabulary. Twenty minutes and one can of Grain Belt beer later I had 147 words.

Some of those terms anybody could probably define, like *chipper* (a deafening machine that, I had been warned, could reduce you to a basket of quarter-sized chips in roughly two seconds if you happened to slip on the slush and fall into the conveyor) or *debarker* (a massive, toothed cylinder that tore the bark off logs and whose logo was a muzzled Great Dane). But others were more esoteric, like *picaroon* (a deft little ax-like tool for grabbing slabs of wood, at least until it was torn from my hands and run through the chipper), *green chain* (where I worked, but not because, as I first thought, I was green), *peavey*, *cant*, *dog*, and *flitch*. I've lost that list along with the memory of most of the more obscure words, but last night (more insomnia, but a bottle of Boulevard Pale Ale this time) I was reminded how each facet of my life has had its own language, its own jargon, and the words I choose at any particular time may show more about me than how I put them together. Enter motorcycling.

So here goes—a few entries from my current motorcycle usage lexicon, woefully incomplete, quite possibly inaccurate, and absolutely arbitrary (and in no special order):

Tank Slapper: Describes a phenomena where your handlebars begin to wobble back and forth, more and more violently until you regain control or suddenly, they stop. This often does not end well.

High Side: Often confused with a "lay down" or a "get off" (which are really variants of the "low side"), a "high side" is probably the worst possible consequence of a "tank slapper", with you leaving the bike over its high side and coming down, well, where are those big piles of leaves when you need them?

Stoppie: The opposite of a "wheelie." Driving down a four -lane through a commercial district, a biker on a YZ1 in the lane alongside my wife and I was doing "stoppies" at each red light, grabbing his front brake at the last second to raise his rear wheel a foot or two off the ground. He eventually got a little carried away and, with his bike reaching a dangerous angle, let up on the brake and lurched awkwardly into the intersection, narrowly missing getting "T-Boned" (self-explanatory). My wife said, "That looks dangerous; is there something wrong with his bike?" "No," I answered, "there's nothing wrong with the *bike* . . . "

Squid: I first heard this one used by a buddy as two kids on sportbikes howled by. "Squids?" I said. "Squids," he answered, "Stupid, Quick, Dead."

Softtail/Hardtail/Knucklehead/Panhead/Shovelhead: They all mean "Harley" to me, but come to think of it, that last one might be a fish.

Boxer: The term supposedly comes from the connecting rods in an opposed-twin cylinder engine, which seem to be boxing with one another, but I always get an image of the "Rock 'Em Sock 'Em Robot" game the neighbor kid would never let me play.

Splines: I used to have a boxer, a mint R65 in fact, and it had splines (at least that's what the manual said). Splines, as I took it, were to be lubricated religiously or things could happen that would be very bad. When I took my airhead in for annual maintenance, I would ask the mechanic, "Did you grease the splines?" to which he would reply (with a roll of the eyes and a note of impatience), "They're fine." I never got far enough into the internal workings on that bike to know if he was just guessing.

Pillion: I was thinking French, but it turns out this term is a Gaelic derivative and was first used to describe a little rug or cushion placed behind a saddle on a horse so a second person could ride (think "pillow").

Panniers: Obviously, the equivalent of saddle bags, but this one really is from the French and comes from a kind of hoop system designed to make a woman's hips look bigger. Do these Givis make me look fat?

Countersteering: Some motorcyclists go through their entire life without reading Hough's *Proficient Motorcycling* or realizing that as they round a sweeping left curve, they're actually turning their handlebars to the right.

Rake/Trail/Caster: Heeding the sage counsel of Mrs. Gross, my sophomore geometry teacher, I'm going to leave these three alone.

Harvest Season: What surgeons started calling spring after Wisconsin dropped its helmet law.

Twisties: What motorcycling, for many, is all about. Opposite: "super-slab." Watch for that far-away look in a motorcylcist's eyes whenever "The Tail of the Dragon" is mentioned (318 curves in 11 miles!).

Cagers: Drivers who will probably never understand the allure of twisties. I think it was Pirsig who once wrote something to the effect that people in cars (cagers) are watching a movie; motorcyclists are starring in one.

Thumper: A one-cylinder bike, so-named for its distinctive sound. If you buy one, be prepared for looks of frank bemusement from the uppity, multi-cylinder boys. My riding buddy refers to my F650 as "the sewing machine," and it pains me to admit I can hear the resemblance.

Road Gator: One of the many banes of two-wheelers everywhere, in addition to potholes, windblown tarps, mattresses, plastic bags, shovels, horse manure, cardboard boxes, plastic water bottles, diapers, bags of garbage, and all the other crap people can't seem to keep from falling onto the road. "Road gators" are slabs of rubber that have peeled off semi trailer tires, only to lie in wait for the next unassuming biker to come along (see "high side"/"low side"). Many riders don't realize that gators have a secondary threat: the wires from cast-off radial belts often are the culprits in flat tires, though they are usually misidentified as staples or nails.

Hard Parts: Anything that drags on the pavement when you get a little too leaned over, such as sidestands, rear foot pegs, or mufflers. Let's face it, your sidestand foot was already too small before you started grinding it down on your favorite twisty.

Basket Case: The best definition I can think of is the mass of parts in my basement that was once a '75 Honda 360. Judging from the way its been cannibalized, the number of acorns still in the mufflers, and the amount of rust in the gas tank, its wheels will probably never know the pavement again, leaving my wife wondering why I keep it at all and easily finding yet another meaning for this term.

As I said, this is an incomplete list. I'm sure with another bout of insomnia and little help I can come up with 129 more of my favorite motorcycling words. What are yours?

Val Immel

12

A Long, Strange Trip

As riders, we all probably attach special meaning to the phrase, "*The journey is the destination*," but sometimes our destinations can change the way we feel about our journeys. This was true in my case on a little jaunt I took last July.

The day started out pleasantly enough, with my loading up and jumping on my bike for what I thought would be a pleasant, relaxed cruise up to north-central Wisconsin for a radio program recording session and then on to the UP for a story I was working on. The weatherman (and my wife) had warned of high winds, but as I swung onto the interstate for the dead- straight run north, there was only a light breeze, and the robin's egg sky was punctuated by puffy white clouds—no problem.

However, by the time I hit a towering bridge over the Wisconsin River outside Wausau, I was being slammed by powerful crosswinds cannonading out of the southwest, broken only by buffeting blasts from passing semis. I was never so thankful to see my exit, which would lead me into the city and to the recording studio. My work there took longer than expected, and rather than ramping back onto the superslab, I decided to continue through the city and try tracing a sparsely traffic-ed two-lane northwest, which if I was lucky, would keep much of the wind quartering at my back.

Once I navigated my way through the city, I found myself meandering through farm fields and forests, but the wind grew even fiercer—not a constant blow, but rather sudden blasts that I judged were hitting at least forty or fifty miles per hour. Given the direction of the wind, turning around would have been even worse than continuing, so I settled in for a wrestling match with the handlebars. There's not a lot a motorcyclist can do in a situation like that; certainly, you have to slow down for every blast of wind, lean into it, keep your grip loose, and flare out your knee on the windward side to stabilize the bike, but at times my only option was to close the throttle and pull over, then cautiously ease back up to speed. There was practically no traffic as far as a little town called Gleason, but soon after that cars started piling up behind me, annoyed, I'm sure, by my erratic maneuvering and my seesawing speeds. Running on empty (in more ways than one), I stopped in after another forty miles for a sandwich and gas, then resolutely set out again. Oh yeah, it then started to rain. It occurred to me that there's a lot to be said for traveling by automobile.

Doubling back on a county trunk when I reached Michigan, I finally made it to a rutted gravel road snaking up to a home situated on a high ridge overlooking Lac Vieux Desert, a huge saucer-shaped lake that is the source of the Wisconsin River. I was greeted by Val Immel, the subject of my interview, and his dachshund, Freud, at the door.

I have known Val for years and in that time had heard intriguing snippets of stories about his family's immigration to America, which had led to this interview. Val's a big guy who speaks with a booming German/Russian accent, and coupled with his ruddy, well-worn complexion and a thick Stalinesque mustache, it's no wonder he's known to the locals as "The Mad Russian." Stressed from the ride, I was jonesing for a beer or one of Val's legendary vodka martinis (chilled Stoly), but as we had discussed on the phone, my main purpose for the visit was to hear the whole story of his family's history, and Val immediately said, "First we talk, then we have a drink."

His story started with the Russian Revolution, when both his parents' families were arrested and sent to Siberia, since they had been landowners in Immelsdorf, Ukraine. With some string-pulling by a Communist relative, they were eventually allowed to return to their homes to become farm workers, but only a few years later, with the onset of World War Two, Val's father, Eduard, was drafted into the Russian army. Captured by the Germans, Eduard chose joining the Wehrmacht's ranks over prison (or worse), but then in the final year of the war, his unit surrendered to the English, and he was interred in a POW camp for the duration. Meanwhile, soon after her husband had been drafted, Val's mother Anastasia, five year old Val, and his baby sister were rounded up by the Germans under the suspicion they were Jewish (they weren't), herded into a boxcar, and shipped off to a work camp. "One of my first memories is of bodies being taken out of the boxcar every morning," Val said.

In 1945, Val's father was freed, and his mother and their children had been liberated from the work camp by the Americans. With a tip on where Val and his mother had been relocated, his father wandered the streets at night, crying out, "Anastasia! Anastasia!" Miraculously, they were reunited; Val remembers his mother was in tears, overwhelmed with joy— she had not heard from Eduard in five years.

Val's tale continued with the story of the family's long journey to America. After winding their way through endless paperwork and interviews in an effort to emigrate to practically any country that would accept them, they were off on a ten-day sea voyage to New York City, where they were told they had a sponsor in Goodman, Wisconsin. Val said, "We had no idea where Wisconsin was, let alone Goodman, but they put us on a train and shipped us out." After reaching Minneapolis, the family boarded another train headed east into Wisconsin. Val remembers that on the snowy ride through the bleak pine barrens of northern Wisconsin, Anastasia exclaimed, "Oh Mein Gott, Mein Gott, we are back in Siberia!"

The family had been sponsored by the Goodman Lumber Company, and though the Immel family faced prejudice for being the community's only "DPs" (Displaced Persons), Val and his siblings thrived and have all been amazingly successful. Val himself went to college, got a teaching degree, and taught German for many years. Always a restless spirit, upon retirement, he took over a bait shop called The Minnow Bucket near Phelps, Wisconsin, which largely due to Val's colorful personality, has since become a local gathering spot.

Rest assured, once the recorder was turned off, the martinis were poured, and Val set about bustling around his kitchen, preparing dinner. Over lobster tail, steak, and home-grown vegetables we talked politics, philosophy, and motorcycles, and the memory of my day's struggles on the road faded.

Later that night, I crawled out of the sack around 3AM for my usual bout of insomnia and walked outside onto Val's deck overlooking the lake. Already worrying about my ride home, I wanted to see if the weather was improving. The wind was still howling, and in the moonlight I could make out luminous skeins of wind-blown whitecaps surfing across the lake. The sky, though, was brilliantly blanketed in stars with ragged, dark ghosts of clouds stealthily racing across to the east. I resolved to not worry about what the next day and my journey back home would bring. To borrow a phrase from The Grateful Dead, life is a "long, strange trip" for all of us, and after hearing Val's stories of struggle, hope, ambition, and perseverance, I was left more determined than ever to enjoy the ride.

13
Chick Bike

One Man's Struggle to Reconcile His Search for the Perfect Bike with His Male Ego

I didn't have to get it. I had a perfectly serviceable Beemer, a faithful 1980 R65. Sure, it had 40K on it, but it ran like, well, any well-maintained BMW. It had everything on it I needed: hard bags, double disks, windscreen, tank bag, even the obligatory Formotion clock, but I felt conflicted. The R65 was twenty-five years old but had exactly three scratches. Being a high school teacher, I was continually waiting for it to get keyed in the parking lot or, just as bad, to fall over because of melting asphalt or its puny sidestand (origin of the three scratches). This would break my heart. It was stately but, to me, heavy, a little loud, and rampant with idiosyncrasies. There was, of course, that little dance all R65-ers have to learn: swing off without putting the sidestand down, then lower the sidestand to leave the bike in a precarious lean. And the famous acrobatic of getting it up on its lofty centerstand, not to mention getting it off. I also heard noises. Was that a front bearing I heard on sweepers? Did the valves always make that much noise? I couldn't deny it's dependability; it had never let me down, but still I started looking around at other guys driving Beemers as old as mine, and they looked old. Was that me? So started my fascination with the F650.

I have owned a number of bikes and must say once you own something from Bayerish Motoren Werke you stop thinking of Milwaukee or Japan. It's not that I'm a snob—that Suzuki V-Strom still beckons to me—but anything else seems, frankly, like a step backward. My pitiful excuse for a bank account, the short stretch of my wife's understanding, and the sale of my R65 would allow me to shop for an older 1100GS or a newer F650, and there the dilemma arose. For my purposes, the daily seven mile commute over, to be kind, "varying" road conditions (I live in the sticks) and my small stature (but I'm wiry) tilted me toward the F650. I had no plans for going from Dakar to Paris, or even California, in the near future. It seemed like a logical choice. However, then I started to talk to my riding buddies. "Chick bike," snorted Ben, who had just come back from the Ozarks on his oilhead. "Do you know it has a chain?" Erik, who is usually quite open-minded, had just acquired a new Gold Wing, courtesy of the semi-driver who had recently rolled over his old one. He narrowed his eyes and said, "One cylinder? Is this for you or your wife?"

Why was it a chick bike? To its credit, BMW is one of the few cycle marquees that features women riding their bikes, instead of posing on the saddle backwards in a thong. And, in their brochures, often it was the F650 they'd be riding. Granted, it's the lightest Beemer, at around 410 pounds or so, and has a lower inseam, but it sure felt manly enough when I took my first F650GS for a spin. I decided to do some research.

Any present owners of 650s who haven't visited F650.com are missing basically everything. I was directed there through the BMW MOA site, and after hours spent perusing maybe one percent of the information there, I must say it has to be the definitive site on this bike. There are seven pages on changing oil. There are ten on windshields. But most important, at least to my male pride, there were trip stories. Guys, GUYS who did Boston to Alaska, twice, with camping gear, two up! (In fact, it's considered the bike of choice for the AlCan, since everybody up there speaks Rotax.) Four corners guys, Iron Butt guys, San Fransisco to New York in ten days guys. This might be a bike chicks (okay, I'd never actually use that term in mixed company) could ride, but it sure weren't no "chick bike."

I started looking around for a deal (the IBMWR site is great, and most importantly, free). But I didn't tell my buddies, except Ralph. Ralph is the guy I ride the most with, and I felt Ralph could handle it. Ralph is non-judgmental. He's retired. He bought an old Airstream just because he likes them. He listens to all of my notions, squints his eyes, and nods. If he wants to wear the same canvas pants three days in a row, he does. He drives an orange and white-tanked Triumph Bonny with black fringed saddle bags. His daughter calls it "that gay bike." This amuses him. He smiles and says nothing.

I finally found a prospect five hours away in Minneapolis. It was a "Classic" F650, 1999. After that, BMW ushered in fuel injection and some other changes. The owner had bought it for his wife (I don't usually mention that) so she could come along on his sojourns down the River Road on his RT. She got pregnant and didn't feel she'd be riding for quite a while. Ralph and I filled a thermos and headed north. It was red. My jacket is red. Obviously, that was a sign. Heated grips, Givi bags, centerstand, a decent windshield, and a throttlemeister—I started signing over money orders. Ralph went for a walk.

Plated and titled a week later, for a maiden voyage I took the 650 on a quick, 300 mile sweep through southwestern Wisconsin, which is about as close as you can get to bike heaven. (If you don't believe me, ask Peter Egan.) As we carved through Wildcat State Park, the bike seemed to be calmly saying, "Are you sure you don't want to lean over more? 'Cause you can, you know, I'm just saying, I've got more before you're anywhere near my hard parts . . . " We cruised the straights smoothly, with the bike only politely suggesting fifth at sixty. We poked through Amish country and tooled up a few gravel roads to break out my pack rod and exploit some prime brown trout hiding places. For the final leg home to central Wisconsin, we traced the Wisconsin River Valley with county trunks. Unfortunately, a cold front was moving in with a vengeance, and we had to contend with thirty to forty mile per hour winds. That wind, frost heaved blacktop, and irrigation pivots with an uncanny ability to douse us conspired to end the trip on a sour note, but I donned my rain gear, plugged in Steely Dan, and the 650 purred right through. We were friends.

Just above the F650 emblem on my bike there is the word *Katalysator*. Rusty on my German, I figured it was some sort of nickname for this model, and I started calling her "Callie" for short. Since then, I've learned *katalysator* means "catalyst" and probably promotes the bike's catalytic converter. But I still like the term: the bike takes me where I want to go, when I want to go, and has already been the catalyst for all kinds of adventures. Since the F650 and I have become one, I think I have finally overcome any feelings of its inadequacy. If I go a day without a ride, I feel incomplete. All things considered, for me, for right now, it is the perfect bike. If it's some people's idea of a "chick bike," so be it. From now on, I'll simply adopt Ralph's strategy: smile, say nothing. I think I know something they don't!

14
HEAD CHECK

So, there I was, sitting in my daughter Sarah's tiny Ford Fiesta, patiently waiting for a red light to change. Adelle was crooning from the CD player, and I was carefully avoiding any head bobbing or lip synching which might suggest to anyone looking that I was getting into it, when—BLAM!—I was rear ended. I won't reveal here the four-letter word I shouted, but the daydream-y mood I had been feeling a moment earlier had instantly fled, replaced by full-on, fist-clenched road rage. I threw the little car into park, kicked on the four-way flashers, flung open the door, and jumped out, to do what I had absolutely no idea.

Miraculously, there appeared to be no visible damage to the rear of Sarah's car. I turned my attention to the car that had now backed off, an old, orange-ish Chevy Cobalt, its nose a mixture of black scuffs, dents, amateurishly applied bondo, and spray paint. This clearly wasn't the car's first "incident."

Still boiling mad, I went to the driver's side, again with no thought as to what exactly I was going to do or say and no thought as to how I would react if the other driver was bigger, angrier, or in all probability, younger than me.

She looked to be all of eighteen years old, a petite kid not much over five feet; no weapons were in sight, but her cell lay on top of her thigh, obviously in its texting app. She was smiling.

"Sorry!" she said cheerfully.

My anger melted into exasperation—this could be my own daughter—I felt myself slipping into Dad Mode.

"Just tell me you weren't using your cell phone." Definitely Dad Mode.

"Nah, I wouldn't do that," she lied. She appeared completely calm, unruffled, as if this kind of thing happened all the time (and from the looks of her beat up car, maybe it did).

I went back between our cars to survey the damage, traffic piling up behind us, the stop lights already having cycled through green and back to red; the honking would start soon. I had no script for this. I couldn't see any dents, scrapes, or cracks, so no need to trade licenses or call the police, right? But somehow I needed some kind of closure. I returned to her open window.

"Well, I guess we got lucky this time."

She shrugged her shoulders and grinned. "It doesn't matter; this car's a piece of crap anyway."

I got back in my car. . . . doesn't matter . . . car's a piece of crap . . . That's it? Was there any remorse? This wasn't closure; she hadn't even seemed embarrassed. But I guess I could see her point, maybe this wasn't a big deal. The Fiesta appeared to be okay, no one had gotten hurt—no harm no foul. But, as the light changed and I resumed my drive home, I was suddenly struck by the thought, "Wait a minute, what if I had been on my bike?"

If I had gotten bumped like that on my motorcycle, I undoubtedly would have been pushed into the intersection where cars in a steady two-lane stream were turning left. I may have lost control of the bike, going down and plowing into (or sliding under) any one of those oncoming vehicles. But then again, maybe not.

When I'm on a bike approaching a light, as a rule, I'm generally nervously watching my six, tapping my brakes, waggling the bike a bit, and looking for emergency escape options, just as I've been taught. It's possible I might have avoided this accident. On the other hand, apparently my only strategy when I'm in a car is to space out and pretend I can sing "Hello." Is it possible I'm a better rider than a driver?

My mind began playing back all the stupid things I've done in a car. When I was sixteen, I remember one late night when I was dropping off the bass player from the band I was in after a gig. As he got out, he issued the popular dare, "Penny for a patch?" Not being one to shy away from any challenge to my frail male ego, I revved my dad's '65 Impala until it screamed for mercy and then dropped the clutch, cleanly snapping off the driveshaft. (The trailer full of amps and speaker columns hitched to the rear may have been a factor.) A year later on a moonless night, I just couldn't resist finding out how close I could come to death by seeing what our four-barrel 383 Dodge station wagon could do on a deer-infested straightaway through a cranberry marsh (answer: ninety-five miles per hour). Still later, refusing to slow down for an ice-covered road, I managed to perch my Gremlin perfectly at the top of a five-foot snowdrift, all four wheels completely off the ground. In my defense, neuroscientists believe that the prefrontal cortex (the part of the brain that thinks about the consequences of acting like an idiot) isn't fully developed until humans are in their early twenties. So there!

Lately, my brain is having different issues, and the blunders I make are less dramatic: missing exits, following a bus onto a pedestrian mall, or wandering onto the shoulder as I spill coffee, drop a donut, or fiddle with Sirius. (Fortunately, my wife, "my helpmate," is now there to promptly point out each of these infractions and share them in detail later with all our friends, coworkers, relatives, checkout clerks, random passers-by, etc.) The list of these driving "oversights" is much too long and much too embarrassing, but it's hard for me to remember boo-boos I made on the bike. An old timer who keeps a rusty Virago in his carport once told me, "Riding a motorcycle makes you a better driver." I'm not so sure about that.

When people tell me they're interested in getting a motorcycle, I'm usually not very encouraging. Riding a two-wheeler can be very hazardous to one's health; I don't want the responsibility for somebody getting hurt. And when riders start telling me about all the things they do in the name of safety, my response is usually, "That's great, but if you really want safety, stop riding a motorcycle." There's no getting around it: motorcycling is dangerous, and survival demands I stay alert and smart. Driving a car seems to leave me lazy and dimwitted. That young lady in the Cobalt taught me something worth considering: I need to be better at both.

15

How to Buy a House

My wife and I have recently been going through the process of selling our house and buying a different one. It's been a bit short of what I would call a pleasant experience, much more akin to journeying through Dante's fifth or sixth circle of hell. Muddling through offers, counter-offers, contingencies, inspections, showings, and the truckload of paperwork has been mind-numbing, though my wife persists in cheerily referring to this phase in our life as "A Grand Adventure."

What's this got to do with motorcycles? You'd be surprised. When it came to selling our house, I'd been patiently informed that to prepare for showing it (called "staging," I learned), the pre-eminent principle, at least according to HGTV, is to "reduce clutter." Apparently, this extended to getting my Beemer out of the garage, since, it was reasoned, stabling my bike at a friend's house every time we had a showing would transform our skimpy, one-car garage into an expanse suitable for a U2 concert. After four or five showings, I got tired of all this shuffling around and somehow was able to convince my better half that keeping a BMW in the garage would only enhance our prospective buyers' opinions of us as sellers with discriminating tastes, a lofty sense of style, and an uncompromising appreciation for quality. Though all family photos were to be removed from our walls to facilitate a buyer's ability to "see themselves in their new home" (another HGTV commandment), I insisted on leaving up my "BMW 1933 GERWINNER DER INTERNAT SECHSTAGEFAHRTS TROPHAE" poster—again, taste, style.

Looking at homes to buy was another matter. In case you haven't heard, in many cities it is a blistering hot market for houses. Since the pull-back from the overly generous financing schemes about ten years ago and the consequent decline in home building, there are lots more buyers than there are sellers. In fact, after a few disappointing incidents where we weren't quick enough on the draw, I began to think the only way to find a house would be to sit in the car with the motor running, ready to tear off toward a new listing as soon as it hit the web.

But we did get to look at a few homes, and it quickly became obvious that my wife's and my lists of "must haves" were distinctly different. My wife was preoccupied with things like "closet space," the mysterious "kitchen triangle," and something called "open concept" (a phrase which doesn't mean what I hoped it might).

I had different standards, most notably among them, where would my bike live? Call me eccentric, obsessive-compulsive, or just plain weird, but it's my custom to keep my bike in the basement through the long Wisconsin winter. Maybe it's the effect of a garage's temperature fluctuations and condensation, maybe I can't stand the thought of a BMW banished to the caste of snowblowers and lawn mowers, or maybe I just like being able to look at a bike while the snow piles up outside, but my understanding realtor (Gold Wing owner) raised her eyebrows, pulled me aside, and whispered, "So, a walk-out, then?"

With each showing, while my wife methodically checked for soft-closing drawers, I searched for a closet worthy of my hoarder's collection of helmets, gloves, jackets, rain suits, boots, and all the gear that populates my panniers. Against which wall would my seven tiers of painstakingly organized issues of *BMW Owners News* and *Motorcycle Consumer News* go? Would the garage support some serious farkling? And what about the driveway? A severe pitch was a deal breaker.

Long story short, we eventually made an offer on a home. Apparently its kitchen triangle is sufficiently equilateral to stave off starvation, and the *feng shui* of the living room is *shui*-y enough that visitors won't shriek in horror.

And yes, it's a walk-out

16
CITY LIFE

As faithful readers of my humble excuse for a column may recall, my last installment was about the prospect of moving, selling our house in the sticks, and moving to a house in a city. Where we used to live, not only could I usually identify the owner of the infrequent vehicle coming down the road by its sound, but I could often predict where the driver was probably going. Eight AM? The high school kid from the farmhouse to the west going to his summer job on his moped. Five-thirty? The snowbirds from next door headed into town for their take-out. As I said, it was the sticks.

Well, now most of the boxes have been unpacked, the furniture has been arranged, I've met the neighbors, and we're almost adjusted to life in the city. Almost. I still have to remember to check the blinds before changing clothes, my wife has to remind me to close the garage door at night, and my daughter still asks, "Now, are we taking our keys out of our cars?" I'm doing pretty well on resisting the urge to pee in the backyard, though.

Basically, it's been a bit overwhelming, and my adjustments on two wheels have played no small part. Take traffic lights. Months ago, there were few, and I could count stop signs on one hand on my way to the grocery or work. Now, I seem to have a knack for arriving at reds as the first in line, and guess what? The lights sometimes never change. Apparently, the street sensors in Eau Claire, Wisconsin, don't recognize my majestic GS as a living, breathing entity. As in many states, in Wisconsin it is legal for a motorcyclist to run a red light after waiting at least forty-five seconds for a change, if it can be done safely, but this still feels like something I might end up explaining to a traffic officer. Other riders have suggested revving the engine, leaning the bike back and forth, and one made the dubious suggestion of putting the sidestand down, dismounting, and pressing the pedestrian button. My technique so far is to look for a tell-tale groove in the pavement where a sensor may be buried and try to stop on top of it. (On left-turn lanes it may be one car length back.) Barring that, I try motioning for a vehicle in back of me to pull up tight on my rear. I've found there is not a hand signal for this that is not open to misinterpretation.

And then there are the distractions. Accustomed to scanning for deer, turkeys, and the occasional opossum, navigating through a university town there are a lot more gorgeous—um—distractions. And even more dangerous, lots and lots of drivers plow toward me with zombie-like stares, with cell phones plastered to the sides of their heads. Suburban intersections here are marked with a system ranging from two way stops to four-ways to unmarked, which could best be described as "whimsical." And of course, noise. Being a newcomer, whenever I hear honking I figure I'm the reason.

But probably the biggest change in my riding habits since moving into the city is the fact that I ride less. There are more than six big-box stores within fifteen minutes of me now, and a cute par-three golf course beckons less than a half-mile away. This new realm of convenience ironically makes riding a bike in full gear less convenient. A romp from my old place for the Sunday paper offered a half hour of fresh country smells, ever-changing scenery, and twisting, deserted roads. Now, an errand for a gallon of milk means stop-and-go traffic, treacherous motorists seemingly bent on killing me, and a nagging concern about my bike's security in the parking lot. However, glorious Driftless Area roads lie just ten clicks to the south, and life in the city has given me a new appreciation for gearing up, getting out, and exploring them.

17
IT'S US OR THEM

When my wife and I moved out into the sticks about thirty years ago, we looked forward to savoring the peace and quiet and living where the wild things were. Little did I know my new life would soon become dominated by an epic struggle against the most fearsome of country horrors. That's right, mice.

Our first encounters with the forces of evil started in the house. At night we'd hear occasional marching and munchings coming from the attic—not too bothersome—live and let live, right? But then they grew bolder in their night-time patrols, and some—I guess their Kamikaze unit—started falling down between the studs in our walls. Thus began a nightly cycle of their scuttering up and falling back down, ending with my wife cowering under the covers and me in my underwear feverishly prying back paneling, drilling holes, and probing around with a flashlight and barbecue tongs to try extricating them. This skirmish escalated into decade-long, heroic campaign of traps, poison, and a painstaking search to seal up every conceivable point of infiltration. Finally, the border, I thought, was secure.

In my city-bred naiveté, however, it didn't occur to me that next the platoons of mice would turn their attention to our vehicles. My introduction to this occurred when, while getting an oil change for my wife's car, the mechanic came out into the waiting area to show me a yucky-looking lump of felt, mouse droppings, shredded tissue, and leaves.

"What's that?" I asked innocently.

"Well, it used to be your air filter."

I did a more thorough search when I got home and found the engine compartment had apparently become a warren of nests, acorns, leaves, and sunflower seeds. I cleaned it all out and zip-tied a trap and some d-Con under the hood. The mechanic had suggested fabric softener sheets and moth balls, so I systematically mined the car underneath the seats, in the glove compartment, and in the trunk. It seemed to help, but again in my innocence, I didn't realize the heathens would flank my advance.

About that time I had made my one and only feeble foray into bike restoration, purchasing an abandoned 1975 Honda CL360 Scrambler for a dollar and storing it in my shed. Anyone who remembers that bike probably shares my fondness for those cool upswept pipes. My dreams of returning the bike to action faded when I discovered those pipes are just big enough to permit determined legions of mice to load in acorns. But somehow not big enough to get them out.

Soon after that retreat, my son talked me into a week-long trout fishing expedition to Alaska. We left my truck in Minneapolis, and when we returned it would crank but wouldn't start. We smelled gas. With the help of a shade tree mechanic (who incidentally used his shade tree to hoist the bed off my pickup), we found mice had eaten through the fuel line just above the tank. One day and about five hundred dollars later, I was back home and, the next morning, jonesing for a cycle ride. I noticed a few shreds of paper toweling underneath my R 1150 R. Popping off the seat, I was presented with a virtual mouse barracks, not to mention a few chewed-through wires. Crap!

I instantly got on the horn to my go-to BMW mechanic, and he suggested replacing the wiring harness.

"What does that entail?" I'm often such a babe in the woods.

"Entail? Um, we'd pretty much disassemble your entire bike, and you'd write us a check for $2,500."

I went to the hardware store for spade connections, solder, electrician's tape, and twenty of their best mouse traps. I was lucky the mice had left enough wire for me to re-establish connections. My mechanic said BMW used a soy compound in the insulation of their wires, which explained the mouse's appetite for them. I built batteries of traps, five to a board, and began baiting them with peanut butter, but it was too hard maintaining them, so I wound up developing a process where sunflower seeds were hot glued to the trap triggers. Vigilance, ingenuity, casualties.

But the onslaught continued. Becoming obsessive about checking under my bike's seat, I found droppings ON TOP OF THE DRYER SHEETS. Clearly, the enemy was evolving. I needed a bigger gun and, after a thorough reconnaissance, realized the only spot without mouse leavings in my garage was where I stored fertilizer. Ah, could that be the enemy's kryptonite? Back at the workbench, I carefully began fashioning darling little sachet pouches of dryer sheets and Scotts Weed and Feed to seed throughout my bike. But then a buddy, visibly trying to be diplomatic, pointed out that some fertilizer is flammable, maybe even explosive. Probably not the kind of final solution I was looking for.

So, after thirty years, the battle rages on. The mice attack seems to have abated, but I refuse to become complacent. Yesterday, as I checked my traps, I saw a chipmunk. It had a dryer sheet in its mouth.

18

PUSHING THE ENVELOPE

TO RIDE OR NOT TO RIDE, THAT WAS THE QUESTION...

I was torn. I had a four-day weekend and an offer from my son to guide me to some of his favorite early season trout streams. He lives in La Crosse, Wisconsin, on the Mississippi; I live on the other side of the state. I could take the pickup and really load up on gear, even throwing in a care package for him, *or* take my F650, which would mean barest essentials, great mileage, and well, you know, more fun. So what was the problem? It was Wisconsin. It was March 18. The weather man looked uneasy. The steel-gray sky looked like snow.

I hemmed. I hawed. I piled my gear in the garage. I decided, well, why not load up the bike, just to see if it's even feasible? Two travel rod tubes, waders and boots, fishing vest, net, rain gear, one change of clothes, camera, three granola bars, a second-hand copy of Gierach's *Trout Bum*, toothbrush and deodorant, plastic. Packing looked do-able. I looked at the sky again, old oatmeal gray. The dash-mounted Formotion thermometer was nudging thirty-five degrees Fahrenheit. It was 1PM; not going to get any warmer. I could call and see what my wife thought, but there certainly was no mystery there. Better to call her after I arrived. I threw on the tail bag and opened the Givis. I was committed.

How many times have you started a trip thinking, "Is this really wise?" and "What exactly am I trying to prove?" It was one of those. I shifted up tentatively. I rolled on the throttle, countering, "What's the worst that could happen?" I suppressed the persistent image of me and a shiny red motorcycle sliding off a banked turn into some snowy pines.

I had, after all, done stuff like this before. When I was in college, tired of being wheel-less all winter, I had hitched home to get my Honda 350 out of dry dock one March. I had to set out on the hundred miles back to school by six the next morning to make my ten o'clock news writing class with Dr. Polk. Everything was covered with a heavy frost. My mother looked doubtful; my dad appeared smug, as if convinced his initial suspicion about me had finally been confirmed: I was, indeed, an idiot. Either I was dumber then or the gear wasn't as good, because, despite duct tape around my face shield, a winter parka, and sorel boots, I began shivering almost as soon as I got on the highway. I started pulling over every twenty miles or so to pry myself out of the saddle and beat my arms together. Windshields were for sissies then; fairings didn't even exist. I'm sure I considered hitting the coffee shops or even turning around, but Dr. Polk was legendary for accepting no excuses short of hospitalization, not to mention holding students who cut class up for public ridicule. By the time I coasted stiffly into my apartment's parking lot, I was shaking violently but at the same time feeling strangely peaceful, detached, and more than a little confused. ("Hypothermia" hadn't entered my vocabulary yet.) I stopped, put my feet down, and just stood there straddling the bike as it continued to run, trying to remember complicated things like how one would go about turning off a motorcycle, or how, having turned it off, one would get off the bike without having it fall over on top of oneself. I looked down with wonder to see the inside calves of my rain pants melted to my jeans, the result of hugging my legs in so tightly to the headers.

As if trying to move through heavy syrup, I remembered the function of the sidestand, silenced the engine by stabbing at the kill switch, and began fumbling for my apartment key. Making a trail of clothing to the bathroom, I turned the shower to hot and curled up on the floor of the stall. A half-hour later I was still shaking but could sort of remember who I was and why I wasn't going to get an "A" in News Editing 255 anymore.

But now, something like three hundred years later, things seemed positively luxurious compared to that jaunt on the Honda. I was snug in layers of fleece, Gore-Tex, and Kevlar, and heated grips and hand guards kept the feeling in my fingers. A seventeen-inch windshield lifted the wind chill up to the crest of my helmet. Had I gotten softer or smarter?

But there were still those clouds . . . those clouds. Wispy threads of what I knew were snow squalls were feeling their way down, lower and lower. At the seventy-mile mark I felt I had earned a piece of homemade pie and a couple cups of black coffee at Connie's Country Café in Babcock. I was the only one in the little place, which was fine, since my pants, coat, helmet, backpack, gloves, and other gear took up two tables. I'd recommend the apple pie ala mode (they warm it up for you without asking).

Suited up and outside again, I pressed the starter, and simultaneously flurries appeared. "Flurries I can deal with," I said into my helmet, as I settled in for the sixty-mile dead straightaway down 173. I screwed down the Throttlemeister at sixty-two and settled back. Straightaways like that one foster a certain Zen-like state for me. You're trapped with your own thoughts, forced to get reacquainted with someone you may have been neglecting for a while. Among other revelations, it occurred to me what a change in roles this weekend presented. My son would be the host, feeding me, shepherding me around, saying things like, "Fish here" and "Do you need to take a nap?" Basically, he would be more like the parent, and I the wayward kid, showing up on his improbable motorcycle.

At Sparta (a fitting coincidence) things got a bit more, well, Spartan. Big, fifty-cent-sized flakes came down in a sheet. My windshield and arms turned white, but I was able to keep my face shield clear as I eased down to thirty-five. At least the flakes were still melting as soon as they hit the road. I soon started getting the "What was he thinking?" look from oncoming drivers. That was a pretty good question, I thought, but then a convoy of Humvees out of Fort McCoy rumbled by, and I had the feeling some of those guys would have gladly traded places.

What was I thinking? Was this some kind of challenge, some kind of meaningless mid-life charade to stave off early bird specials and senior citizen discounts? Was pushing this envelope going to prove I was as tough and daring as any kid half my age? Maybe I was just desperate for a good ride on a motorcycle. I plodded along to the first convenience store and daintily steered in to re-evaluate. I looked miserable but realized I felt pretty okay. I munched a Butterfinger, ignored the smirks from other customers, and waited for the squall to pass.

I must have passed through three or four more snowy sections in the final thirty miles of my trek, but having chosen back roads, I could take it easy or pull over whenever I needed to, and even in these less than ideal conditions I still could enjoy carving into Wisconsin's "coulee country." I pulled into my son's driveway feeling tired and happy. I turned off the engine, swung the sidestand down, and leaned back on the tailbag to savor a moment that I think only a rider knows. The old man still has it, I thought. Just then my son pulled in next to me, home from work. He gave me a blank look of resignation and shook his head. Dad would never grow up.

19
SUNDAY PAPER RUN

I'm sure it's a dilemma familiar to all news-junkies such as myself: continue to flip and fold your way through good old-fashioned newsprint and ink or go digital and subscribe to your favorite paper or news service. My dad was a newspaper man who subscribed to two or three daily papers and on Sundays made the weekly pilgrimage to the drug store to pick up papers by the pound from Milwaukee, Madison, and the Twin Cities. With my family of six each pulling out their favorite sections, our living room was usually carpeted ankle-deep with news, sports, features, and comics.

I did leap headlong into the twenty-first century though, fixing my news habit with a subscription to a state paper that even includes the Sunday edition and yet . . . I still can't seem to break my habit of making the Sunday Paper Run. My motorcycle may have something to do with that.

It's pretty tempting to just hop in the car and drive the five miles to town for the paper; heck, I could probably just do it in my slippers and pajamas, but instead I push myself through the tedious ritual: ear plugs, helmet, riding jacket, armored gloves . . . carefully back the bike out, hop on, and hit the starter—it immediately begins to feel worth it.

The country roads are deserted on Sunday mornings, and I'm free to worry less about traffic and take in more of the view. In late July the flora and fauna are in a headlong crescendo of life. A pair of fawns gambol obediently after their mom across the road and into the safety of the woods, cranes in the alfalfa pause from their breakfast to glare as I roll by, and the first tentative groups of blackbirds have started to buddy up on power lines. The morning sun sparkles off the burdock, queen ann's lace, and dill in the ditch, and the air feels fresh-scrubbed and is scented with windrowed alfalfa. I stand up on the pegs to let it blast over me.

As my speed picks up, my week of making the world safe from dangling modifiers, faulty pronoun reference, and apostrophe abuse seems to fall behind. Now, I can play, and I tilt the bike into a long sweeper, searching for the perfect line of entry, apex, and exit. The bike is on rails. The feeling I get streaming smoothly through a long curve at sixty miles an hour is a little like hitting that sweet spot with a five iron, smacking a chunk of oak just right with a splitting maul, or what I imagine it's like schussing a black diamond slope. Needle-sharp focus, a quickening heart rate, tension and release.

After picking up the paper, I turn the wrong way out of the convenience store—a quick detour is in order. A sublime shot up through the lazy curves of Highway 49, a pause on a bridge over the Tomorrow to check the black shapes of trout, and some dainty maneuvering around the frost heaves of Isaacson Road, and it's homeward bound.

As I coast into the garage, I can already smell cinnamon rolls and coffee. I almost forget to pull the paper out of my tank bag. Is that what I was after?

20

RUNNING THE MINDORO CUT

Few avid motorcyclists haven't heard of the famous "Tail of the Dragon" near Deal's Gap, North Carolina. Its 318 curves spread over just eleven miles have made The Dragon a legendary mecca for riders. But in Wisconsin, we have our own version: the Mindoro Cut.

Located near La Crosse, between West Salem and Mindoro on Highway 108, the Cut sits in the heart of Wisconsin's Driftless Area. The last glacier bypassed that part of the state, though its gushing runoff sculpted southwestern Wisconsin into a maze of towering ridges and deep, twisting valleys. Back in 1907 farmers around Phillips Ridge found it too steep to climb with crops for the railway in West Salem or milk for the Mindoro Creamery, so they had to take the "long way round." Under Governor Bob LaFollete's Good Roads program, the state and area land owners paid workers

$1.25 a day to chisel a cut through the ridge. To their dismay, contractors found they had underestimated the task. Rather than sandstone as they had thought, they struck a hard, dolomite dome ten feet down. After two years, using only horse-drawn wagons, wheelbarrows, picks, shovels, and a little dynamite, workers had carved out what, at seventy-four feet deep and twenty-eight feet wide, is the second deepest hand-hewn cut in the Western Hemisphere. It still ranks as the oldest cut that has remained unimproved, and in 2007 it was added to the National Register of Historic Places.

But, amazing as that might sound, it's not the Mindoro Cut's history that attracts motorcyclists, sports car enthusiasts, or even bicyclists. It's the curves, or to use rider jargon, the twisties. Starting on level ground and winding up and over at 1,300 feet, riders get a chance to thread their way through twenty or thirty snake-like bends and switchbacks. Though you can find plenty of pretty hairy videos online of riders pushing the limits of their skill, most riders enjoy the cut for the challenge of finding a smooth line through each bend, an elegant ballet of countersteering, lean, and throttle. The scenery's worth a leisurely look too. Pausing at the turnout marked by a historical marker, you're bound to witness an intermittent parade that runs the gamut of two-wheelers: older couples on gleaming BMWs talking excitedly into their helmet intercoms, grim-faced sport riders planning the apex of their next line (hopefully on the right side of the double yellow), grinning bikers rumbling by on Harleys, or even perky-colored scooters, their riders just having a blast.

My recommendation: Whether you're a rider or what we call a "cager" (on four wheels), check out the Mindoro Cut. But take it easy on your first run. Enjoy the sights. Think finesse, not fast. This is no race track, and you never know who (or what) might be around the next corner. Hey, even the Tail of the Dragon has a thirty mile an hour speed limit. And you know you're going to want to turn around at the bottom and go right back through.

21
THE DEER DILEMMA

Deer. Can't live with 'em, can't hunt down every single one, wrestle it to the ground, and cut out its still-beating heart. Okay, that may be a bit harsh. (Where's my "Some-readers-may-find-the-following-text-troubling" sticker?) Actually, my feelings about the furry four-legged menace are, to use the parlance of the day, "conflicted." I live in the boonies, battling daily to keep thick woods from swallowing my house on three sides while the fourth faces eighty acres of delectable field corn. And I live in a county that leads the state in deer kill numbers every year, a state that is always in the top ten when it comes to deer strikes. So, deer are constantly around, and I must admit I enjoy seeing them; they're lovely creatures with fascinating habits and abilities, but after a summer of dodging them on the highways, many evenings during October and November will find me shivering in a tree, trying to harvest one for the table.

I've been responsible for the untimely demise of something like sixty deer, though you could say with four of them it was more by their doing than mine. Of course, under today's legal leanings, I was probably at least ten percent guilty by just being on the highway when those four decided to commit suicide by car. In one case, a group burst from a cornfield that bordered the road, another made a beeline out of the woods and into the headlights of my Toyota. The other two ran into the sides of my vehicles, leaving the image of a doe's wide-eyed expression in my passenger window forever etched in my memory.

Living in Wisconsin, I've heard lots of questionable tips on dealing with deer. When I was just learning to drive, a buddy's father insisted the best thing to do when you see a deer by the roadside is to continue on at the same speed, convinced slowing down, speeding up, and keeping a steady pace all carried the same odds for an accident. A one-time girlfriend told me if you can see a deer's eyes reflected in the dark, that means it sees you and will not cross your path (I hope she still doesn't believe that). And then there's that woman who called in on a radio show to suggest the answer to deer-car collisions was to place deer crossing signs on roads where there is the least traffic, so they would choose to cross there (search YouTube: "Please move the deer crossing sign"). You'd think, at the very least, riders and drivers here would have developed some kind of universal signal to warn oncoming vehicles of deer in the ditch, but as far as I know, there is none.

I do see cars and bikes festooned with deer whistles, and who am I to question their effectiveness? I've heard lots of people claim they've never hit a deer after installing them; of course, they haven't hit any unicorns, aliens, or zombies either. If nothing else, they can't do any harm and may provide peace of mind; however, in my experience, though the bugle-shaped, "silent" variety are great bug catchers, I can't say I've seen much evidence of their effect on deer. This summer I was given a handful of "Deer Screamers" (deerscreamer.com), a new approach in that these whistles make a tone audible to humans and deer alike once a bike hits about fifty miles per hour. They also have an innovative, double-barreled design that doesn't trap insects. The MOA members I distributed them to said they couldn't see any definitive results; however, inventor Bill Pereca claims the sound generated by Deer Screamers seems to "freeze" deer, making it less likely they will bolt across the road. There does seem to be some video and anecdotal evidence of this, and Deer Screamers have been distributed to State Troopers in at least two states to try to create a meaningful data sample, but obviously, it is pretty tough to really tell what deer are or are not reacting to, and I have to wonder if any solution can ever really be "proven" to work, or even if it's really possible to do a reliable scientific test.

Though there have been some close calls, no deer strikes on the bike for me yet. And, given the deer numbers around here, I can attribute that to, well, basically sheer luck. Sure, I'm fairly good at predicting what kinds of roadsides on my usual routes are most likely to sprout a rogue animal, but let's face it, if a deer is determined to leap into my path, there's not much else I can do about it. Of course, slowing down and wearing good protective gear are always good ideas.

As I've said, I'm conflicted. Deer are a dangerous hazard, but I'd miss them if they weren't around, and collisions are not the deer's fault. They were here first, after all, at least by three million years longer than we've been upright and riding motorcycles.

In my view, there is no silver bullet when it comes to finding a solution to deer strikes, (though certainly lead bullets lessen the odds each fall), but there is a silver lining: staying alert for deer is just one more dimension that adds to the exhilaration of the singular, in-the-moment motorcycling experience.

22
NOTHING SLIMEY OR CRUDDY ABOUT THE SLIMEY CRUD RUN!

Okay, let's get one thing straight right off the top: I'm not a big fan of group rides. Maybe it's my inherent '60s cynicism about any kind of group-think, or maybe it's just the anxiety of rolling down an unknown road amongst a pack of riders of unknown proficiency. Even if I'm invited to a run for a good cause, frankly, I'd sooner stay home, watch golf, and send in a donation.

Which is why, you might ask, would I venture forth on something sounding as unlikely as "The Slimey Crud Run?" Actually, it's what the Slimey Crud lacks that first attracted me. Check this out: no real sponsor, no swapmeet, no beer tent, no bike dealers, no worthy cause, no kiosks of accessory venders, and other than a selected date and obscure location, not even a set route! Sure, there's a Slimey Crud website (www. slimeycrudrun.com), but it even bills itself as "The Official Unofficial Website of the Slimey Crud Run." Add to that the prospect of ogling more than 2,000 bikes of every marque imaginable and dusting out winter's cobwebs with a ride through some of the most scenic and twistiest roads in the Midwest, well, in short, I was in.

So, as the first Sunday in May broke clear in Wisconsin, I joined a trio of MOA members for my first "Slimey Crud Run." According to writer Gary Carpentier, the run was founded in the seventies by the "The Slimey Crud Motorcycle Gang," a group of University of Wisconsin grad students who were spoofing the biker gangs portrayed in a run of movies and media coverage then. Given a few mentions by legendary *Cycle World* columnist Peter Egan (who grew up in the area), the run has festered and grown into one of the Midwest's biggest bike gatherings, attracting riders from at least five different states, always on the first Sundays of May and October.

As soon as we jumped off the superslab spine of Wisconsin called 90-94 and headed southwest we were on the state's rollercoaster called the Driftless Area (that portion of the state which escaped the last glacier). Before entering Pine Bluff, the jumping off point for the SCR, we stopped for a scrumptious breakfast buffet and some fellowship with the Madison BMW Club where we were given some pointers about The Run, including a caution about the local gendarmes who were said to be out in force. Then, topping one last hill, we coasted into Pine Bluff around ten and waddled our way down a main street flanked on both sides by a mile-long lineup of bikes of every description.

Ducati, KTM, Cagiva, Moto Guzzi, Triumph, BMW, Yamaha, Suzuki, Kawasaki, MZ, Aprilla . . . I was in total sensory overload before I even got my sidestand down. And then I realized there were even more bikes in side lots: a cute little Honda 350 Scrambler, an immaculate /6, a Rocket here, a Valkyrie and a Vincent there—who had the BSA with the café bars and what appeared to be canvas fairing? There was a fair share of Milwaukee's finest, but few of the chopper genre; instead, the ranks swelled with platoons of Beemers, from fully tricked out GSs to LTs with dashes festooned with farkles worthy of a space shuttle. There were also fleets of cunning sport bikes, joined by a heavy contingent of café racers. Amidst an occasional throaty wail from somebody's streetfighter, there was the constant hum of rampant rider talk, and grins were as common as gear shifters.

If there is any structure to The Slimey Crud Run, the idea is to follow this chaotic (but oddly, fairly peaceful) rendezvous in Pine Bluff with a sprint to an even smaller town, Leland, about thirty miles distant. But, of course, true to the SCR's nature, how you get there and how much you want to slog the county trunks and township roads is your business (well, possibly one of the County Deputies', too). Jim Riederer, Madison Club member, had laid out a circuitous route for us that led us through an hour-long labyrinth of snaky roads, with only a few other bikes in sight. We arrived in Leland around one, where, it seemed, there were even more bikes. Again, it was a little disorienting to have been tilting through the coulees one minute then suddenly be thrown back into all bikes great and small the next, but the camaraderie I had seen in Pine Bluff had been magically teleported to Leland. And there were cheese and sausage sandwiches, locally made brats, burgers, lots more bike talk, sloppy joes, and Sprecher root beer. It was sunny, I could hear a Ducati clutch rattling by, the ominous snarl of a new S 1000 RR, and the classic blat of an old, pea-shooter Bonny. Bike Heaven.

At the end of the 300 mile day and home again, my wife wanted to know would I do it again? Let's see: every bike I could possibly imagine on display, Deal's Gap quality roads threading through stunning scenery, the opportunity to commune with thousands of riders cut from the same cordura cloth? I'll be back.

23

How to Read a
Motorcycle Magazine

Read at Your Own Peril

Okay, I know this is a motorcycle magazine. I know you are reading it. Obviously, you know how to read a motorcycle magazine. But, if you are one of those who (like me) is truly obsessed with reading everything and anything connected with motorcycles (especially in the winter months), you have probably begun to suspect that there may be certain hazards, certain pitfalls, associated with your habit. So with apologies to the publishers of all those magazines to which I'm hopelessly addicted, let my scribblings be a warning of what you, the pitiful slave of all things bike, can expect:

1.   The Blank Look. You've seen it. At parties. Around the watercooler, the bar, or just about anywhere you talk to people not of our persuasion. Their eyes narrow, possibly dart back and forth, as if looking for an escape route. Hard as it may be to believe, some people just aren't interested in a comparison between the dyno ratings for the 2003 versus 2008 Hayabusa. In fact, you may have to explain what a "Hayabusa" is, and unless you mention the connection to Ben Roethlisberger, their sudden need to call the babysitter might lead you to suspect they don't really care what it is. Who can begin to explain the lack of enthusiasm for a spirited debate on the true origin of BMW's roundel or the initial shear rate of Castrol versus Mobil 1? Being unable to resist injecting motorcycling analogies into conversations isn't going to help: "Oh yeah, the adjustment to the prime rate, well, that's just like the time I tried to remap my Multistrada after hanging on that Akropovic, kept getting that surge around 2,000 rpms . . . " (Listeners begin giving each other knowing glances of desperation.) And of course there's no better way to wind up talking to the tropical fish at a party than to fall into one of your tirades about road hazards: "The driver never even looked, except at his cell phone!" (Listeners offer a quick prayer that their cell doesn't choose that moment to ring.)

2.   Over/Understatement. I don't want to say that magazines aren't always truthful, but any seasoned reader would probably agree that just about any article should be approached covering the front brake lever of skepticism. For instance, when reading a review of a new bike in a mag that accepts advertising, it might be wise to remember who's paying to keep the lights on, the word processors booted up, and that article in your hands. Also, when a writer is testing a bike (already feeling generous for having the whole day to tool up and down Highway 1) his opinions may be, let's say, "shaded." A line like "the ergos weren't quite right for my height" may be translated as "The first of my twelve

chiropractor appointments began shortly after my run to San Simeon." Or: "Some riders may have an issue with the heat emanating from the left manifold." Translation: "Aerostich voided my warranty, stating their suits should not be worn while welding." Also, in a bike review, clichés like "a rocket on steroids" sound much better to readers (and marques) than lines like "capable of getting you a speeding ticket in any state in the union." (Incidentally, any prospective writer for moto-magazines should know "on steroids" can be attached to just about any noun for an always startling effect. For instance, "A tankbag—On Steroids!" or "a keychain—ON STEROIDS!")

3.   Ads. Those girls and guys in the ads for leathers, helmets, and pipes? No, sadly, they aren't included in the purchase price, and no, you won't even see them at the dealership, nor will you begin to even faintly resemble them if you buy the product they're hawking. Which, of course, raises the question of the need for the mysterious, oft-advertised pheromones, and is there any relationship between them and pervasive ads for radar detectors and that stuff that makes your license plate hard to photograph? I have to admit I'm a gadget junkie of the highest order, but do I really need chartreuse flames for my fuel tank? Well, probably. A multi-tool/flashlight that translates my voice into morse code? Why not? Color-coordinated reservoir caps? Of course! Can I possibly continue to make my seven mile commute to work on County Trunk B without hearing a Bluetooth update on my tire pressures every seven seconds? No, obviously I can't.

4.   Becoming a One-Percent-er. Be aware that, of all the information you absorb from reading bike magazines, ninety-nine percent may turn out to be totally useless. Forever. So, let's say after all these years, you finally discovered the definitive last word on the bore/stroke ratio of that 1975 Honda CB200 you used to own? Not only that, but you breathessly read how both plugs fired on every upstroke. How

could you have not known that before? The fact that possibly none of this information may come up in Trivial Pursuit or even *Jeopardy* may leave you asking, "Who's writing those questions, anyway?"

5.   Lest We Forget. And, of all the countless bits of useless information you absorb, rest assured ninety-eight percent has a respectable chance of being forgotten. And of that remaining two percent, let's face it, if memory retention studies are any indication, at least seventy-five percent will be remembered incorrectly. Ever pick up a two-year old copy of your favorite bike mag? (Don't stop to wonder why you're saving them.) Did you read that travel piece about Nova Scotia before? The pages are crinkled, the type's a little smudged, hmmm, didn't you resolve to ride to Halifax once? How could you forget first reading about the switch from female-slider front ends to male-sliders and the subsequent rise in the natural flexural frequency of clavicle wear?

6.   The Wishing/Buying Continuum. Not only will you spend much of your time reading information you'll never use, probably forget, or remember incorrectly, but many of the bikes you intently read about have about as much chance of sitting on a cycle stand in your garage as Tiger Woods practicing chipping on your front lawn. Don't get me wrong, I never miss a story about any stunning one-off museum piece meticulously-hand built by little old men in Milan or a fire-breathing board tracker from the Deep South hand-hammered out of an International Harvester combine, but in my heart I know I'll have to be satisfied with a bike that starts every time, runs as long as I ask it too, and leaves me just enough in my checkbook to make the house payment and take my wife to dinner.

So, am I against reading motorcycle magazines? Hardly. In fact, it's no accident that the end of each month finds me hovering around the mailbox, waiting for the next new issue. But notwithstanding my wife's puzzling suggestion to, in her words, "get a life," I must admit it's a curious and remotely dangerous compulsion. You have been warned.

24

THE CHINESE CONNECTION

Often called "one of Wisconsin's best kept secrets," Tom Zatlonkal's Motorama is an eye-popping museum of over four hundred vintage cars and more than a hundred motorcycles, not to mention a "motor pool" of all kinds of military vehicles and a "boneyard" of many other classic rides. After catching a brief clip about this mecca for lovers of all things internal combustion on the local news, my riding buddy, Ralph, and I stoked the GPS and spent an hour or so drilling down through state highways to county trunks to the gravel driveway entrance of the museum marked by a 1950s' police car resting on the bed of an army Deuce and a Half.

Motorama is also known as "Alfa Heaven," since it has the largest collection of vintage Alfa Romeos in North America (Bob used to race them). Almost all the Alfas and the rest of the hundreds of cars and military vehicles on display have been restored to showroom spec, and though the stable of restored motorcycles is smaller, there is also a "bike barn" of over one hundred bikes waiting for some tender loving care.

After meeting Bob and wandering off through the massive car sheds, outdoor military vehicle line-up, and on a boardwalk through a forested boneyard of ancient cars, I found a line of meticulously restored bikes. I soon spotted one I checked off as a classic Beemer, but on closer inspection I realized it was a bike I had never heard of, the Chang Jiang.

Tom Zatlonkal, an effusive host, caught up with us at that point and had an instant connection with Ralph, who it turns out, shared Tom's hometown of Elmhurst, Illinois. Ralph coincidentally had probably bought his first vehicle, a gorgeous 1964 Chevy Impala SS Convertible, from Bob's dad, just prior to getting his friendly letter from his local draft board. Bob has many stories to tell, but his tale of procuring the Chang Jiang was a particularly interesting one. It seems when he heard of the "Chinese BMW," he just "had to have it," and that started an odyssey lasting six years and one trip to the Nanchang factory. The Chang Jiang was manufactured primarily for the Chinese army, and prior to the '80s, government policy forbade selling military equipment to foreigners. With lots of persistence and even more paperwork, Zatlonkal finally procured one for his museum. Ironically, once China opened trade to foreign markets, production of Chang Jiang came to an end; however, Chang Jiangs are still available and they have a small following of enthusiasts, who admittedly prize their "Chinese Beemers" more for their rarity than their reliability.

The Chang Jiang is derived from the 1938 BMW R 71, the last of the side-valve Beemers. Before capturing an R 71 tooling line near the end of WWII, the Russians were already producing copies of the R 71, which they called the IMZ M71 and the M72 ("M" for "motorcycle army"). Stalin had purchased five BMW R 71s via a trade agreement in 1938 that allowed Russian engineers to reverse-engineer the predecessor of the Ural. Many countries and manufacturers had tried to copy BMW's flat-twin design, including Harley-

Davidson, which modeled its XA prototype after R 71s that were captured by the allies in Africa. By the '50s, the Russians judged the R 71 design obsolete and sold the entire tooling line they had confiscated to the Chinese, who began producing Chang Jiangs (named after the Chang Jiang River, also known as the Yangzte) around 1960.

There are three iterations of the Chang Jiang boxers: the M1, a side-valve, six-volt model; the M1M, with an iffy reverse and electric start; and the M1S, which upgraded to overhead valves with the help of German engineers. With a 750cc air-cooled engine and shaft drive, most Chang Jiangs were fitted with a side car and produced about twenty-two horses, top speed in the fifties. Before the Chang Jiang, the Chinese were building a German Zundapp KS600 knock-off. Since the CJ750 was built for the military, it was made with heavy-duty materials, though, according to today's owners, the same quality did not extend to the small bits like gaskets, filters, and bushings. Production of the Chang Jiang 750 ended in the late 1990s, and they could be purchased as military surplus during that decade. Independent specialists continue to build bikes from stockpiles of parts. The Nanchang factory is not out of business, however, and a prototype of a CJ650 with a parallel-twin and sidecar was unveiled in 2017.

Central Wisconsin's Motorama/Alfa Heaven is open May through October, though the museum opens its own sports bar for special holiday parties and events with live entertainment. The forty-acre compound also hosts probably the Midwest's largest military show, featuring military vehicles, a swap meet, and re-enactor encampment (August 10-11 in 2018). The Motorama Auto Museum's motto is "You have to see it to believe it," and after seeing scrupulously restored cars from marques ranging from Austin to Zaporozhet and motorcycles from CZ to Chang Jiang, I'm glad I did.

For more information and a map to Motorama/Alfa Heaven, visit Alfaheaven.com.

25
"The Disease"

Right about the time my desperate longing for a Schwinn Stingray started to wane, my fascination with anything that ran on gas began. Those rear wheel slicks, butterfly handlebars, and swooping banana seats on Stingrays (and on the twenty-inch bikes my buddies had commandeered from their little sisters) just couldn't compete with the Hurst-shifter-ed, late-'50s Chevys, rumbling GTOs, and new Ford Mustangs that were perpetually taking laps up and down our little town's main street. And though my own father had been showing symptoms for years, somehow I had been oblivious to his own enchantment with cars and his consequential addiction to buying new ones almost every year—the habit my family casually referred to as "The Disease."

I'm still not quite sure how he did it. We were a single income family of six, and though Dad may have been getting some deals as a result of managing the advertising on the local paper, I've got to think he was making ballooning car payments for all of his adult life. One day he might roll home for lunch in a lavender Chevrolet Malibu, a year later it might be a Volkswagon Karmann Ghia. The variety of makes and models I watched rotate through our dilapidated garage as I grew up had no limit: a bronze Impala with three on the column (my dad was a strict adherent of manual transmissions, no matter how unwieldly), an AMC Gremlin (two concrete blocks in the rear as optional accessories), an El Camino, a Blazer, a Pacer (rolling greenhouse), a Toyota Tacoma—by the time I was in college, I fully expected to see a new vehicle every time I came home for break. When I would say, "New car?" my dad would answer with a shrug of surprise, as if to say, "What do you mean? Of course it's a new car." I don't think my mother, the saint, actually approved of my father's obsession, but I guess, with her characteristic sigh and a roll of her eyes, she had resigned herself to it as an incurable, if fairly harmless, affliction.

And apparently susceptibility to "The Disease" is genetic. Both my brother and I seem powerless to resist the siren song of new vehicles, no matter how feeble the rationalization or how thin our wallets. Some milk was spilled in the back seat? We obviously needed a mini-van. The road is late getting plowed one day? Let's go look at four-wheel drives. Tires and brakes need replacing? A trade-in would simply be "a wash," right? Yes, I even once talked my wife into splurging on a new, enormous crew-cab pickup so our family could go camping. (We did go. Twice.)

This disorder I've inherited is not limited to cars. I'm now on my twelfth motorcycle, even with an eighteen-year hiatus while I waited for my kids to grow up. Among those, I've had four BMWs—an old one (R65), a small one (Funduro), and a bigger one (R 1150 R). But all of those bikes were purchased "pre-owned," so with the prospect for an end to my riding years no longer a distant abstraction, this year I went looking for something in the "New Inventory" realm.

Buying a new BMW isn't quite the exhilarating little dance I've come to expect when buying a new car or even a used bike. Pestering all the dealers within a three hundred-mile radius, I found salespersons basically have their hands tied on asking prices. There may be a promotion or some wiggle room on accessories; if a trade's involved, possibly some room for haggling, but all of that finesse I'd picked up from years of car deal diplomacy was of little use.

Though the new bike bargaining process didn't offer much excitement, the browsing and test rides did. I rode every model that seemed to fit into the narrow parameters of my inseam, riding habits, and checkbook. Having been away from new bikes for a while, I was in awe of features like self-canceling turn signals, steel braided brake lines, gear indicators, and tire pressure monitoring, and as salespersons rattled off strange new acronyms like DWA, ASC, ESA, and TPC/RDC, I nodded knowingly, as if I had any clue what they were talking about.

When I found the bike that seemed to fit me best, it seemed like suddenly I had passed the point of no return. My wife (another saint) was supportive, though her comment, "Well, it's probably the last bike you'll ever buy . . . " was a little disconcerting. My boss at *Owners News*, Bill Wiegand, sagely counseled, "Ron, if you don't buy that bike, the terrorists win." And though there were all kinds of valid reasons for walking away (a perfectly good V-Strom in the garage, an educator's salary, a failing washing machine, and a looming tax bill), I pulled the trigger, this time on a 2016 Mineral Grey Metallic BMW F 700 GS. What can I say? It's not a character flaw, it's a disease.

If this bike is on a trailer
it is stolen.

26
TRAILER TRAUMA

I saw a sticker the other day that read, "IF THIS BIKE IS ON A TRAILER IT IS STOLEN." I had to wonder how popular that sticker is, since there are perfectly good reasons for trailering a bike. For instance, maybe the hypothetical owner did some hypothetical work on his final drive, only to discover a day later an unidentifiable but pretty important-looking part lying on his garage floor. Maybe the hypothetical owner finally found someone to buy that hypothetical 1975 Honda CB200 he'd tried to nurse back to health, and delivering it was the only way to ensure the bike would still be running when it got there (again, hypothetically speaking). Or just maybe the hypothetical rider, out of his eternal, loving consideration for his wife, chose to trailer his bike to a hotel where she could get a spa treatment and watch HGTV. (While he fondles carbon fiber key fobs in a vendor booth at a certain national rally twenty miles away.) So, there are good reasons to trailer a bike; however, I avoid trailering like I would a natural disaster because, well, that's often what it's been for me.

My first inkling that trailers and I don't mix emerged when I took delivery of my first BMW, a 1980 R65. The bike had been tuned and immaculately repainted, down to the pinstriping. The dealer ran it expertly up onto my four by eight stake trailer using his skinny aluminum I-beam for a ramp, and we tied it down. When I got home, I was too anxious to ride the bike to wait for a buddy to come over and help and decided I could handle the off-loading myself. I had a ramp I had fashioned from a two by twelve, but for some reason that escapes me now, I had swung down the jack on the trailer tongue and unhooked the trailer from my truck. The reader may be well ahead of me at this point.

I put up the sidestand and, both hands on the bars, started to back the bike toward the rear of the trailer's bed. It's possible I was paying more attention in sixth grade science to Debby Wolinsky's new ponytail the day Mr. Krohn patiently explained the wonder of fulcrums. Or possibly I was just too excited to consider the elementary physics of the situation. Or possibly I'm often an idiot. But when the bike's rear wheel approached the end of the trailer, the whole trailer, of course, tilted up, the tongue pointing into the sky like a 105mm howitzer.

So there I was, desperately squeezing the front brake with the bike poised at a forty-five-degree angle, praying that my nosy, know-it-all neighbor, Ralph, wouldn't drive by and see this unfolding fiasco, while at the same time praying my nosy, know-it-all neighbor, Ralph, would drive by and rescue me. If I released the brake and continued backing the bike, I knew as soon as the rear wheel was off, the trailer would seesaw back down and there'd be no way to avoid dropping the bike. The immaculate bike. After panic finally subsided, it dawned on me I could put the bike into gear, get the sidestand down, and step away. I grabbed a step ladder to hold trailer's tongue up, and then was able to get bike off, but somehow the burning desire to immediately go for a ride had vanished.

Years later, I had sold a Funduro to a young lady from the Twin Cities. The plan was to meet her halfway across Wisconsin, where we would off-load the bike so her boyfriend could ride it home. Again, in my anxiousness to get the deal done (and turn the cash around on a beckoning R 1150 R), I decided to load the bike myself. Using my trusty two by twelve and a plastic step stool, I figured I could use the bike's motor to power it up. Again, the reader may be miles ahead of me here. As I began to walk the bike up the ramp, carefully feathering the clutch, the stool I was stepping up on toppled over, causing me to twist the throttle grip, hard. The bike wheelied onto the trailer (dragging me along with it) and climbed over the side rails but luckily hung up on the frame, as I went over the side. The sounds of the whine of the engine and the crash must have been terrible, since my wife came running out of the house to find me lying on the ground. Gas was dripping, my pants were ripped crotch to cuff, and yes, there was some blood. My wife did her best to look sympathetic, but anyone could see her delight over the new my-husband-the-moron story she'd be able to share for, apparently, the rest of our lives.

There are even more just as humiliating disasters—forgetting to lock the coupler latch, flat tires, melted bearings, a little mishap involving a parking garage barrier lowered between my truck and trailer—but you get the idea. If you see my bike on a trailer, it's probably not stolen, it's probably terrified.

RESERVED PARKING

FOR
MOTORCYCLISTS
ONLY
(If they can
survive this
parking lot!)

27

WELCOME TO MY NIGHTMARE: THE PARKING LOT

When on my bike in a parking lot I'm typically as jumpy as a cat in a room full of rocking chairs. And it isn't that I'm worried about that oil patch or coolant puddle the last vehicle left or my bike falling over because of the spongey asphalt (I'll never park a bike without a kickstand foot or pad again!). It's because I fear for my life.

But apparently most drivers don't feel that way. According to a survey done by the National Safety Council, sixty-six percent of drivers feel comfortable talking on the cell phone while driving through a parking lot. Fifty-six percent feel comfortable texting, and fifty percent feel comfortable using social media, watching videos, or writing email. If that wasn't troubling enough, at least forty-two percent said they would video chat while they cruise for an open space or search for the exit.

Those people are nuts. The insurance industry claims one out of five accidents happens in a parking lot, and as a result of the 50,000 plus accidents that happen there every year, the National Safety Council reports, on average, 60,000 injuries and fifty deaths. NO ONE should feel comfortable in a parking lot, especially when you consider the looming wild card of demographics: as of 2010, the US Census indicated those citizens sixty-five and older represented the biggest chunk of the population in terms of size and percent, and they're getting older, many obviously on the cusp of that awkward intervention with their kids over shredding their licenses and donating their vehicle to the Car Talk Vehicle Donation Program.

A little story to wit: A neighbor of mine who is at that watershed age parked his manual-shift Toyota on an inclined lot in front of a Kmart, but forgot to yank the emergency brake as he went in to shop. His car rolled backward all the way through the quarter-acre lot, across four lines of traffic, up and over the curb, and into a dealership lot on the other side, where it gently came to rest against a power pole. Miraculously, not a single car or pedestrian had been touched. When he was done shopping and emerged from automatic doors, he thought his car had been stolen, then noticed the pulsing squad car lights down across the highway.

But don't think this is another curmudgeon-y rant against cagers; pedestrians are often just as much a hazard. The number of injured "distracted walkers" (a phrase unknown to most as late as 2000) doubled from 2004 to 2015 and is expected to double again by the end of 2016. And what parent hasn't ever had a breathless moment when one of his or her children stepped out between parked cars without looking? In the words of Deborah Hersman, head of the National Safety Council, "There's a lot of inattention out there."

Distracted drivers, aging drivers, zombie-like pedestrians, and children, not to mention the usual idiots you find behind some steering wheels . . . all these physical hazards coupled with a false sense of security and an "anything goes" traffic mentality have the minefields known as parking lots giving "adventure motorcycling" a whole new meaning.

Personally, I can recall four or five close calls with cars in those vast seas of blacktop. What can we do? Experts on safety like David Hough suggest keeping your eyes moving, looking for exhaust coming from parked cars and flickering tail or backup lights, covering your brakes, anticipating escape routes, and only rolling along as fast as you feel safe. I'm not above standing on my pegs and toggling my auxillaries to modulate in the biggest, most congested lots. Call me superstitious, but I also stay out of mall lots on the weekends before high school proms.

On one of my last commutes of the year I had to navigate the parking lot of a big box grocery store. As I was cautiously threading my way through the lanes to the exit, a blue SUV suddenly squirted in front of me. My saving grace was that I could see the driver and had noticed she had never even glanced in my direction as she pulled out. As I followed her to the street, I noticed the oversize bumper sticker fully spanning the hatchback panel: "IN GOD WE TRUST." That may be a fine guiding principal for her, but when it comes to parking lots—really anywhere I'm riding—I prefer my own motto: TRUST NO ONE.

28
NO WORRIES

I needed a good book to read, but I was out of new stuff, so I went to my bookcase for something worth a second look. Scattered among the shelves were a good number of motorcycle tomes, many of them contenders: Peter Egan books, Paulsen's *Zero to Sixty*, *Storm*, Bill Stermer on the R 100 RS, Pirsig, Pierson, William Least-Heat Moon. But my finger finally came to rest on a well-worn copy of Ted Simon's *Jupiter's Travels*. What better way to spend a snowbound evening than sharing a trek around the world on a motorcycle?

For those who haven't yet read it, the story opens with Ted running out of gas on a dirt track after taking the wrong turn in India near the end of his trip. His complete lack of concern about a breakdown like this and his blind leap into the adventures it led to really set the tone for the whole book. The author's memoir soon flashes back to the beginning of his journey, and about eighty pages in we see Simon in a different light. Tracing a rutted excuse for a road in eastern Africa, he describes a growing sense of dread about his fate on the trip, and he begins to fantasize about the countless things that could go wrong—crashes, injuries, mechanical failure, extreme weather. For some reason, the contrasts in Ted's attitudes from the beginning to the end of his odyssey made me consider my own mental state when riding.

I have to admit it, I'm a worrier. Maybe it's because I'm such a disaster with mechanical issues, or maybe it's just in my DNA (my brother used to spend hours driving around at night when his heebie jeebies got to him; my dad drank martinis). Like Simon in the early part of his trek, once my thoughts are cloistered in my helmet I think I tend to obsess a bit over what could go wrong. Is that the sound of a valve going south? Does that rear tire feel low? My tailbag's still there, right? Is that a rain cloud? Re-reading Simon's book, I started thinking back to my own mini-crises and how, in retrospect, maybe things going wrong might just be all right.

Take, for instance, when I panicked as my Honda 350's rear wheel began squirming around with my first flat. Sure, it was an inconvenience, and it meant talking one of my college roommates into chauffeuring me around on his little Suzuki dirt bike for a patch kit, but how else would I have learned (from the same roommate) the nuances of setting the final drive chain tension correctly? About twenty years later a drywall screw stranded me for a while at a BMW dealer in Green Bay, but while I was waiting I met a GS owner who was in for a bent rim. He explained to me the concept of "target fixation" (he had failed to avoid a chunk of four by four on the highway). I remember him describing his early-2000s GS (a bike I knew practically nothing about at the time) as "heavy and slow" but still the "last bike I'll ever want."

Coming back from the MOA National in West Bend, Wisconsin, my buddy and I pulled into a little town for gas, and as soon as I started up my F650, white smoke began pouring from the engine. I was in a panic, but my buddy,

Ralph, sagely conjectured it was coolant and as long as I could keep the overheat light from coming on, we could probably make it the few miles to Mischler's BMW in Beaver Dam. Fortunately, they were keeping late hours because of the rally. In that waiting area, Ralph and I met a fellow traveler who had stopped in for a new clutch cable. His bike, buried under all sorts of leather fringe, getback whips, a yard of sheepskin, and a roll of canvas tarp, was a fairly ancient-looking airhead, and his devotion to the bike led to my thinking maybe I should own one someday. (I did.)

The tables turned a year or two later on a trip headed for an BMW Riders' Association event in Michigan's Upper Peninsula when Ralph's Bonneville threw a spoke through its rear tire and he had to call for a trailer. I ended up ditching the rally idea and tracking down a childhood pal who had just mustered out of the air force where he "flew" a fueling boom on a B-52 over Iraq. On the deck of his lake cabin we feasted on venison burgers, drank Molson beer, and caught up on twenty years of separation.

The point of all this, and what is more clear to me now, is I've resolved to stop worrying (or at least to worry less) when I'm in the saddle. As someone once told me, there are only two rules when it comes to motorcycles. Rule Number One: Something will go wrong. Rule Number Two: You can't change Rule Number One. Almost every breakdown, inadvertent detour, or weather problem I've encountered on a motorcycle has led to memories I never would have had if I had been driving a car and memories I never would have had if everything had "gone right."

29

MY AFFAIR WITH
"THE POOR SISTER"

No matter what kind of bike I've had over the last few years, my wife always refers to it as "your girlfriend." Well, last spring I got the itch for a new "mistress" and did quite a bit of speed-dating with all kinds of different bikes. I settled on a new 2016 BMW F 700 GS, and if we had a Facebook profile, it would read, "In a relationship."

I must admit, I was first drawn to the F7 by her looks. Dual floating discs up front, kind of a Ducati-esque trellis frame, the typical GS wide bars and upright seating arrangement, cast aluminum wheels, and a quality finish were all flirts that had me ogling. Of the two color schemes available then, I preferred the Light White, but I soon found most dealers only stocked one F7, and they most often chose the Metallic Grey model for their showroom floors. Nonetheless, it's no wonder that the bike in either skin draws longing looks at gas stations and parking lots.

I read a lot of motorcycle magazines, and of course, just about every word in *BMW Owners News*, but rarely, except for possibly a corporate press release, is there ever a mention of the F 700, so as my infatuation grew, I did what I guess most do now when they're seeking a new mate: I Googled her. I found that, if the F 700 GS is mentioned at all on a website, forum, or blog, it's sometimes referred diminutively to as "the baby GS," "the poor sister," or "entry level." The lack of attention for this bike and disparaging attitudes seemed a little odd, since I also learned the model was very popular in Europe and is often bought in fleets for guided tours, training, and for rentals. I decided to keep an open mind and do some road tests.

I guess my favorite feature of the mid-range GS is its size. Probably ninety percent of the time I spend on a bike is commuting about thirty miles over country roads, county trunks, and four lane slab and poking around in stop and go traffic and parking lots. The F7's lower seat height, moderate weight (467 lbs. fueled), and narrow frame make it the perfect partner for this. Over our first season together, it has given me around sixty mpg, and I have never felt it was underpowered for seventy mile per hour highways (approximately 75 hp @ 7300rpm), though even with six gears, it can get a bit buzzy at faster speeds than that. The "700" in its moniker is actually a misnomer, since the engine has the same displacement as the BMW F 800 GS (798cc); the F7 has simply been detuned a bit, since it's designed for easy riding and not for roosting off-road.

As I was shopping for a new road mate, I also rode the similar-sized V-Strom DL650 and the Kawasaki Versys, but with the F7's tank below the seat, I was first struck by how much more stable it was in the wind than the taller profiled Suzy and Kawa. Anyone comparing the 700 GS with its nearest competitors will probably be struck by the price difference. The F 700 GS is not a cheap date. I got mine for about $12K, including tax and license with an optional BMW Comfort Seat thrown in (like many F7 owners, I strongly recommend this option). The V-Strom and Versys are both nice bikes, but I like my BMW dealer and service department (Tytler's in DePere, Wisconsin), and the F7 I'm going steady with came with the Premium Package, including luggage racks, center stand, heated grips, stainless brake lines, a number of tech options (ESA, ABS, ASC), and adjustable pre-load and damping. Also, the dash features dual trip meters, gear indication, temperature, and tire pressure. None of the other bikes in its class offered all of those features at that time.

I know it's a big mistake to try to give your love a make-over, but I must confess, "Hello, my name is Ron, and I'm a farkle-holic." Though less popular in the States than its more well-known BMW sisters, one nice thing about the F 700 is that all the biggest aftermarket providers offer tons of accessories that it can be dressed with. For my weekend sojourns I added a Touratech luggage rack and Zega Pro cases—light, pretty, and rugged; they've been perfect. I also mounted a Wolfman Blackhawk tank bag and a Pelican topbox for my camera gear, which still left room for a passenger seat bag and a "Tooltube." For safety, I added Cree running lights on the forks, a decelerometer from Vololights in the rear, and a homemade headlight shield.

As I've found with other bikes of this size that I've owned, finding a windshield that cuts buffeting can be a challenge. The standard F 700 shield looks nice but does practically nothing, and I went through three before I settled on a Madstad, which judging from the forums, seems to be a popular choice. I also tried a number of different handguards, including a used set from BMW, but eventually settled on a set of bike-specific ADVance Guards from MachineartMoto that are the beefiest I've ever seen and offer three configurations for varying weather conditions; they also don't interfere with a "BrakeAway Cruise Control" and a "Helmet Hook." A witness to past bike tip-overs, I fabricated my own kickstand foot, and I also wrenched on some Givi crash bars—my girl's good looks are safe.

Admittedly, BMW's F 700 GS is not a bike for everyone. For one thing, it's not the kind of bike I'd choose to carry a passenger and luggage to Alaska (though I met someone who has … twice … pulling a trailer!). And though it may look like it, it's not suited for anything rougher than a gravel fire road, since it has a smaller front wheel, less travel, and suspension components that are a step down from the F 800, but then again, so is the price. So, despite its aggressive appearance, the F7 is what I would call a genuine street "all-rounder."

During our first season together, the F 700 GS has been a faithful soulmate and has made my daily commute a pleasure and my weekend excursions full of flick-able fun. Make no mistake, I'm a happily married man, but I can't wait to spend another season with my newest "girlfriend."

[BMW replaced the F 700 GS with an F 750 GS for the 2019 model year—a little more displacement, new colors, gas tank moved back up front, among other tweaks.]

30

THE WEAKEST LINK

I've probably been reading too many motorcycle magazines.
The stacks of issues down in our furnace room are teetering,
threatening to become the furnace. I'd recycle them, but I
can't help thinking there's some tiny shred of information
buried in there that I'll desperately need someday. Moreover,
there's a psychological problem as well. Every magazine has
its maintenance section, and I just can't read article after
article on topics like how to measure the sag in your bike with
some sand bags and a few feet of dental floss or how to align
your wheels with a two by four without experiencing more
and more powerful pangs of guilt. The underlying message
of all these stories is that real motorcyclists do their own
maintenance, and I confess, I have done practically zilch.

The trouble is, when it comes to torque wrenches, voltage
meters, and micrometers (whatever those are), I am the
original village simpleton, capable of generating thousands

of dollars of damage with a single twist, tap, or yank of my vise grip (basically my number one tool, when it can be found). However, guilt is a strong motivator. I've lain awake at night wondering if I should try changing my brake pads (and what the heck is "sintering?") or worrying if the bird's nest of accessory wires under my saddle will one day torch one of my favorite body parts. I stare in awe at seductive images of Touratech suspension components. I pretend I understand the formulas for rake and trail.

Is there anything I could do? I began sifting through YouTube videos about maintenance chores simple enough for a Neanderthal. Ever look at those clips? Often the thumbnail for the video sports a buxom young lady in a tube top lasciviously fondling a socket wrench; however, when you open the video, the narrator, can of Bud in hand, appears to have just finished digging his own septic system. His dog repeatedly walks in and out of the shot, and in the distant background we hear his wife calling, "Hey TV star, how about doing a video on cleaning the rain gutters?" But I did stumble across an operation that I felt surely lay within my somewhat limited skill set: cleaning and greasing my chain.

Chain maintenance, I learned, is not only pretty easy, but it is an important step toward extending chain and sprocket life and increasing gas mileage, not to mention giving me something to talk about with a hint of authority at the Wednesday night bike meet. With at least a month before the beginning of Wisconsin's eagerly awaited three day riding season, I systematically gathered my tools and supplies. Short work, since I didn't have any. YouTube said, first of all, I would need a chain brush. Sure, some said, an old toothbrush might work, but is that the tool you want hanging on your pegboard? Off to Amazon. There are all kinds of chain brushes there, but in an unusual concern for quality, I dutifully resisted my usual partiality for "thriftiness" and passed on "economical" models that had reviews carrying phrases like, "fell apart in my hands on first use." I settled on an aluminum "Grunge Brush," just in case my new dedication to DIY would last at least three lifetimes. YouTube experts also counseled to get some kerosene to clean the chain, but all my big box store had was a ten gallon vat, and not seeing a fork lift around, I settled for a quart of mineral spirits. Out of remorse for my compromise, I splurged on a ninety-nine-cent spray bottle.

When it came to oil for the chain, I quickly tumbled headlong into the rabbit hole of bike forum threads where multi-page debates on the best chain oil raged, only surmounted in megabytes and fervor by the infinite opinions (and a few disturbing threats) on the best engine oil. Again at the big box store, I closed my eyes and grabbed a spray can from the lineup of brands. An optional purchase, I learned, was a sort of wheel cozy, which shields the rear wheel and tire from overspray (yes, you can actually buy those), but I just couldn't see the advantage of those over a carefully fashioned piece of cardboard, stealthily scavenged after dark from my neighbor's recycling bin.

My arsenal of weapons assembled, the next afternoon I rolled my bike out to the driveway. No sooner had I hoisted it onto its centerstand when my neighbor strolled over. He wanted to know if I had seen any suspicious individuals poking through his garbage. Of course, I hadn't. I wheeled the bike out of his prying eyes and into the garage. By then my chain brush had gone missing. It only took five dog biscuits and a humiliating twenty-minute game of keepaway through three backyards with my Lab, Penny, to get back on task.

Running the chain through the brush while dousing it with cleaner took just a few minutes, leaving me to wonder why in all the videos I watched the narrators felt the need to be so adamant about NOT RUNNING THE ENGINE to save time during this step. I guess they felt obligated to offer the warning, but even I could see how having your fingers eaten between the chain and sprocket would be worthy of a minor Darwin Award. With a good wipe down with a pile of T-shirts that have mysteriously started getting too tight and a drenching of oil on the now sparkling chain (and on my hands, my shirt, my pants, the floor, my shoes, and Penny), the service work order was complete.

I pulled out a lawn chair and toasted my new-found elevation to the ranks of mechanic, third class, with a frosty bottle of Fat Tire. My guilt assuaged, I pondered my next challenge: rain gutters.

31

So You Want to Ride a Motorcycle

My daughter recently indicated to me she was thinking of getting into motorcycling. Knowing I have a history with bikes, and of course, trusting my advice to the point of worship, she came to me for a few kernels of wisdom. In the hope of getting her started right and possibly providing a path to other would-be bikers, let me share my somewhat snarky advice to her . . .

1.   GO BIG! I know, I know, some people will say start small, stay with a scooter or something you can easily control, something with just barely enough cc's to enter an interstate, but where's the fun in that? Why not buy the biggest, baddest bike you can find? Sure, you may have trouble reaching the handlebars, you may need a step stool to get on, and it may be three or four or five times your weight, but think of the nice

people you'll meet when trying to horse it uphill and out of a parking stall or when the sidestand sinks through the soft blacktop and your bike falls over. And think of the impression you'll make on the state patrol officer as he writes you a ticket for ninety-five mph in a fifty-five zone.

2. GO LOUD! Nothing turns people's heads like a loud motorcycle. Imagine all the irate neighbors, the barking dogs, the crying babies, the hearing loss, and again, the kind officer writing you a ticket for a sound ordinance violation—more date material!

3. SAFETY GEAR, ARE YOU KIDDING? If you absolutely can't let go of the desire to live past twenty, you will probably fall prey to the lure of protective gear, like a helmet, a jacket, boots, gloves, and pants. If you must, one word: *black*. Now this may seem to contradict that basic human need to draw attention to oneself or even seem to infringe on what those preachy safety experts call "conspicuity," since obviously wearing black is the best way to disappear into the landscape. But think of black as the new orange, or at least the new hi-vis yellow, two colors which could lessen your chances of getting hit by a driver who "never saw you" and subsequently deny you a huge insurance payoff (assuming you're around to collect it). Oh yes, a word about helmets: if your police state's philosophy is to take away your God-given right to traumatic brain injury by requiring helmets, just get one of those replica WWII Stormtrooper helmets. Again, great attention-getter, and like loud pipes, they really enhance the image of motorcyclists everywhere.

4. LICENSE, SHMI-CENSE! For some unfathomable reason you may be required to take a ridiculous, multiple-choice test over the motorcyclist manual and maybe even a "behind the wheel" driving test. Are they kidding? A quick check of the statistics will reveal a surprising percentage of uninsured riders involved in accidents also never bothered to get a license. Think of the money they saved for things like loud mufflers, black clothing, and medical bills—it's a

win-win! And all those rules? Forget them, there's really no such thing as "right of way" when it comes to motorcyclists—drivers don't follow them, so why should you?

5.   NO SKILLS, NO PROBLEM! Though "trainers" may differ, piloting a motorcycle is easy, as long as you can do something different with each hand and foot, often simultaneously, while at the same time scanning 360 degrees for wet leaves, dogs, deer, sand, stuff falling out of the pickup trucks, cardboard, oil and coolant spills, rocks, raccoons, skunks, turkeys, branches, and drivers suddenly turning left in front of you. I know, it sounds like a lot, especially since it will be so hard to resist texting as you ride, thumbing through your playlist, and touching up your make-up, but it can be done.

Fortunately, ever since my daughter became a teenager she has probably correctly pegged me as a narrow-minded, cantankerous old curmudgeon hopelessly mired in dogma and whose capacity for sarcasm is only surmounted by his talent for exaggeration. She would certainly guess the five points above are some of the worst advice any prospective rider could be given. As she's learned in the past in other endeavors, when it comes to advice about becoming a rider, it's probably best to read the research, talk to experts, watch videos, get qualified guidance from a certified motorcycle instructor and take everything her old man tells her with a heaping helmet-ful of salt.

32
MOTORCYCLI-FISHER-IST

Is it just me, or are there a lot of motorcyclists out there who are also anglers?

It's not like there aren't a lot of similarities between the two pursuits. For instance, many motorcyclists (especially ones like me) have an insurmountable obsession with accessories and equipment. Did I really need that virgin sheepskin seat pad with anti-slip backing, custom bungees, and optional UVA-UVB resistant coating? Of course I did. Just like I needed that Gore-Tex -treated fishing cap with the drop down neck gaiter, extra-long brim, fly patch, and wind clip. And how can anyone ride without custom-molded ear plugs made from Amazonian beeswax or fish without a titanium-plated Boga Grip? Is it any wonder that Aerostich features not one, but three different fishing kits for motorcyclists?

And let's not forget the veritable goldmine of meaningless, esoteric knowledge that rests in the two vocations. True, few outside of our two constituencies would ever care about this treasury of knowledge (go figure), but nonetheless, there's a certain shared pride among riders and fisher-people in knowing things like the difference between rake and trail, bore and stroke, or the difference between siwash and drop-shot fishing hooks, not to mention knowing the biographical highlights of GS icon Herbert Schek's teen years or why fly fishing god Lefty Kreh is called, well, "Lefty."

But there are less tangible connections too. Who can deny the spiritual feelings of oneness with the universe after a perfectly executed, delayed-apex skewer of a mountain S-curve or a delicately feathered cast of a Hula Popper to just inches from the edge of a lily pad (where it's promptly inhaled by a six-pound smallmouth)? Sure, there are those who like to point out the pointlessness of riding a K bike ninety-five miles for a piece of strawberry pie or casting a two pound musky plug a thousand arm-numbing times without so much as a follow (and calling it a "good day's fishing" at that), but actually, those people, are they even human?

I first made the connection between two wheels and fishing rods when I was in college. A buddy had taken me to a secret fishing spot where our somewhat liberal definition of the phrase *private property* necessitated leaving his car on the highway, ducking under a chest high barrier, and hoofing it down a dirt road for a few miles. The walk was a pain, but the fishing was excellent, and it occurred to me a return trip would be an excellent opportunity to employ my Honda CB350, with which I could scoot under the gate and save myself from all the hiking. I bungeed my spinning rod to my sissy bar (everybody had a sissy bar then) and—okay, you've probably seen it coming—sneaking under the gate snapped off my rod, which I never discovered until I reached the lake. A flawed plan to be sure, but that didn't dissuade me from using my bikes whenever I could to get to more "secret" places, though I was always uneasy about leaving a bike in the woods, out of my sight. Turns out that bike was stolen out of my driveway.

And the skills! Ralph Waldo Emerson wrote he liked people who could "do things," and rider/angler people can certainly do stuff. I've known motorcyclists who can tune spokes as well as Eric Clapton can tune a guitar and can check valve clearances in a motel parking lot, in a driving rain. Fishers can tie a double cinch knot, replace a sheer pin with a rusty nail, and catch a walleye with little more than a pop top and a piece of barbed wire.

But there are some notable differences between the two passions. First, weather. To a piscator, heavy weather can be good: wild fluctuations in barometric pressure can put fish into a feeding frenzy, and some of my fondest fishing memories include days where my rod guides kept freezing up, when sunburn made my nose look like a strip of bacon, or rain fell in buckets. I do have memories of riding in snow, heat, rain, and wind; they are not especially fond ones. And though there's nothing like the satisfaction of tying into the fish of a lifetime, let's face it, nothing compares with pure, head-jerking acceleration.

While writing this piece I asked my better half, "Isn't it amazing how many motorcyclists also fish?" Her answer; "Not really; they're both nuts."

33
REHAB

Early this past summer, my son treated his old man to a golf outing as a birthday gift. I'm a pretty conservative golfer, preferring to stay in the fairway with short yardage swings, rather than spraying all over the course, but by the seventeenth hole my son had shamed me into pulling out the driver and for once letting "the big dog eat." As soon as I made contact, I felt like someone had given me a jolt in my lower back from a cattle prod. To add insult to injury, the ball barely cleared the women's tee.

The doctor's visit, CT scan, and X-ray that closely followed revealed a fractured vertebrae and herniated discs, and so began a summer of ice packs, heating pads, ultrasound treatments, Netflix binging, ibuprofen, muscle relaxers, Vicodin, physical therapy and an umbilical relationship with my Back-A-Line back belt. As anyone who has had back trouble has learned, there is no physical action which doesn't call on back muscles, from a sneeze to tying one's shoes.

On doctor's orders, motorcycling was out (though I couldn't resist taking a short spin, which quickly confirmed why I'm not a doctor), so I had a long, boring drive to the Des Moines MOA International Rally. No one approached me at the gas pumps to ask where I was headed or how I liked my Subaru, and despite my BMW/MOA hat, riders were wary when I approached them at waysides looking for some camaraderie. No leaning or countersteering was required.

On the way there, though, I was thinking about Jim Ford (*The Art of Riding Smooth*) and his advice about re-examining your riding habits. I decided that the rally might be a good time to rehab not only my back, but my riding habits as well, and while I manned the MOA Demo Table, I'd ask other riders about what they thought were their "best practices" when it came to safety while on the road.

Ron Bogucki, a former motorcycle safety coach, was the first to point out that possibly some of my habits might not be so great. For instance, knowing that many car-cycle strikes are caused by drivers turning left in front of motorcyclists, I routinely would toggle my headlight switch dim to bright repeatedly when approaching vehicles turning left or even cars ready to pull out from my right. Ron diplomatically informed me that flashing your brights could be seen as a signal to motorists to "go ahead." Whoops, one habit retired. He also enlightened me about a better habit when looking for trouble. "Bracketing" means breaking the oncoming scenery into sections, targeting one section of a direction, then moving your eyes to another, instead of continuously scanning left and right for danger. He said fighter pilots are drilled to make that second nature.

Dana Conklin advised making a habit of moving around in your lane to attract more attention from drivers, especially when slowing, coming to a stop, or approaching a vehicle looking to pull out. Marina Ackerson, who is approaching her 400,000-mile mark, said her habits include staying out of the center of a lane, usually preferring the left third. She also showed me her brilliant Clearwater auxiliary lights and mentioned she will not ride with any group that doesn't liberally stagger their positions on the highway.

More than one rider I talked to mentioned something for lack of better word I'd call "profiling." I've always made a habit of closely watching what kind of vehicle I'm following, but I don't think I've paid much attention to the kind of "human environment" I was riding through. Extra vigilance is, of course, a good idea in proximity to schools (especially high schools, peopled with inexperienced drivers) and probably hospitals, since ambulances may be around, but what about passing by a Social Security office, or a big box grocery store on senior day? It was even mentioned that dog park parking lot exits were a gold mine for distracted drivers. Bars, nightclubs, cycle and car dealerships—is there any other group I can offend? "Looking for trouble" has a bad connotation, but it makes a lot of sense to me. I think of this not as prejudice, but as prudence.

As I get closer to getting into the saddle again, I realize that the more I learn, the less I'm sure I know.

34
REHAB, REVISITED

In a column I described how a back injury left me with an opportunity to rehabilitate my back and my riding safety practices while I spoke with MOA members at the international rally in Des Moines. I ended by inviting my loyal and presumably countless readers to offer their best practices when it comes to preserving their own skins while on the road. I received some great responses, full of tips that, while possibly not all original or unknown to many of us, certainly bear repeating...

One strategy that came up at the rally, which I, for lack of a better word, call "profiling," generated an email from Bernie Peterson. In addition to paying special attention to obvious potential trouble spots like exits from schools, hospitals, etc., Bernie suggested keeping a lookout for RVs, since drivers may be navigating unfamiliar roads and may be renting their vehicles, thus being new to their operation. By the same token, he looks for U-Haul trucks—again, drivers probably unaccustomed to their vehicles and the area. "Profile like your life depends on it—it could save your life," wrote Bernie. Sounding a note similar to the ones made by safety experts like David Hough, Bernie also suggested riders, while staying on guard for distracted drivers, should consider their own mindset—distraction can work both ways. He added his personal slogan: "Half of them (drivers) are out to get you, and the other half don't see you."

Randall Beecham and Charlie Rohlfing both commented on the ever-present danger of cars waiting to pull out from driveways and side streets. Though it's natural to focus on the drivers' eyes to see if they're looking in your direction, they may be looking through or past you. Randall and Charlie believe in concentrating on a car or truck's tires or wheels. Charlie made a good point when he wrote that detecting movement of an entire vehicle is harder than seeing it in a wheel, which, he contends, "magnifies" the motion. As Randall wrote, "Nothing is foolproof, but if the front tire is not moving, neither is the car."

Like me, Steve Vetter wrote that when he bought a new bike after being off one for two years, he started watching YouTube videos about riding safety. He wrote that one British video he watched demonstrated the "weave" technique, where a rider does a little wander side to side in his lane when coming up on vehicles waiting to turn left or pull out from side streets. Rick Griffith also endorsed this maneuver. Steve wrote, "I'm not sure how effective it will prove to be, but it's fun for certain!"

How to make yourself more conspicuous was another popular thread in the emails I received. James Kennedy was high on Clearwater Lights' Darla auxiliary light system. He wrote that he first noticed the Darlas' effectiveness on a police bike. He wrote, "The Clearwater Darlas the officer had on his bike snapped my attention, though he was a long way off and definitely not in my field of vision." James also recommended adding amber lens covers to any DRLs (Daytime Running Lights), since they add more visibility and safety.

Along with making yourself more conspicuous to oncoming vehicles, Dennis Shaw noted that staying visible to those in the rear is just as important. Because of the narrow signature of a motorcycle, it can "hide" in the profile of a stopped vehicle in front of it. There is a plethora of inexpensive options for additional, inexpensive rear lighting, but Dennis wrote that he even toggles on his emergency flashers when stopped in traffic and cancels them when a car stops behind him.

More than one member wrote me comments that fall under the category of "bike position." Though Glenn Evans conceded his comment was probably out of one of David Hough's books, he wrote that he tries to stay in the left lane when on a multi-lane highway, since it reduces the number of vehicles surrounding him. He added that when in an exit lane he automatically assumes someone is going to cross in front of him at the last minute. Conversely, he watches out for cars in an exit lane to have what he calls "an OH CRAP! Moment" and cut left into his lane.

Following too closely was another tip that relates to bike position. James Patton wrote, "Stay back from traffic and move to an area of the lane where you can get the best vantage point of the situation ahead on the road." He continued, "I'm seventy years old and have slowed my pace . . . the wider following space helps me with reaction time and gives me more information to assess . . . I also see more scenery now!"

Al Bredberg also zeroed in on where he positions himself on the street and highway. "Cars are not my friend—if they do not get near me, they cannot hit me. I have sixteen feet of pavement and use it all. A moving target is hard to hit; I traverse my lane one side to the other in traffic, looking on the inside of a curve, and staying out of the grease strip in the middle." Al added that on an empty highway he stays on the left track to give him a little extra cushion away from anything that might leap out from the roadside. Al wrote he doesn't follow trucks, vans, or "anything that blocks my vision," though when riding at night (which he tries to avoid) he routinely follows a car just outside his low beams. "They'll hit the animals before we do," he wrote.

My thanks to all those who sent me their tips. Their suggestions reaffirmed once more what continues to draw me to riding: there's always something new to learn.

35
WHERE THE LIGHT IS

I'm not crazy about riding my motorcycle at night. Riding at night obviously compounds what can already be a dangerous activity with amplified and additional threats. Your vision is reduced to a single, mesmerizing tunnel of light, and that makes it harder to spot nighttime prowlers like deer, raccoons, and skunks. The armor in your jacket and your helmet can feel pitifully inadequate, and the headlights of approaching cars can be blinding. In the event of problems, you're often alone on the highway.

About half of fatal motorcycle accidents happen after 9PM; however, it's important to note fewer riders are on the road at night. Also, of the fatal nighttime accidents that occur, about forty percent involve motorcyclists with a 0.8g/Dl BAC readings or higher.

But sometimes, by choice or circumstance, we sometimes find ourselves riding after dark. A late meeting, lingering over a dinner with friends, or maybe you're trying to make just a few more miles to the next "Vacancy" sign. Still, despite the elevated risk level, riding at night can be exhilarating: the cool, still air, the aloneness, almost like riding by yourself on a deserted rollercoaster.

I had to do a few miles on a summer night recently, and once again I had those mixed feelings that riding after dark can conjure. The familiar county road seemed a little foreign—corners a little more abrupt, forest edges a little closer. I crested a hill, then dipped down into a valley, the temperature abruptly dropping as I sliced through fingers of fog. Climbing again, I hit a cloud of bugs—some kind of hatch probably—my faceshield peppered with a wave of nymphs. Something bigger splatted into my knee. And then I was suddenly out in the open, hay fields on both sides and a brilliant canopy of stars overhead. Here then was the constant paradox motorcycling presents: ever-present risk weighing against the singular, addictive experiences only riders can know.

A few years ago, a good friend of mine found himself heading home in the dark from his job at a vet hospital in Michigan's UP. He'd worked past midnight in his role as a respiratory tech, and then had to negotiate Highway 2 while trying to avoid out-driving the weak beam of his late '80s BMW R 100 RT. In one of the darkest stretches, a doe suddenly bolted out of a ditch and into his lane. The RT's fairing practically cut the deer in two, and when my buddy came to, he was lying in the road. Carefully doing his own physical assessment, he found himself covered with entrails (to his relief, the doe's) and a jigsaw puzzle of fiberglass shards that had once been the Beemer's fairing. Miraculously, he walked away from that night ride with just a fractured collar bone, but he sold the bike the following month, vowing he was done with two wheels. A year later, he bought the same Beemer back, his bike, body and lust for riding restored. As I said, a paradox.

As I hummed along, it occurred to me that riding at night is not only a perfect illustration of motorcycling's two-edged sword, but it's also a metaphor for advancing age: companions fall away, children take their own roads, dangers lurk unseen in the darkness ahead. But there's also that new urgency, immediacy in life, that growing older (and riding a cycle) generates—an enhanced appreciation for living in the moment.

Experts tell me there are things I can do when I choose to ride at night: wearing ATGATT, reducing my speeds, focusing more on situational awareness, and keeping brakes and clutch covered. I've also taken to carrying a pair of yellow-lensed, fit-over glasses that give me better night vision. Checking the aim of the headlight(s) is a good idea, along with upgrading to HID or full LED lighting, and statistics seem to indicate adding good auxiliary lights decreases the likelihood of an accident, though use of those might just reflect higher levels of rider experience and attention to a host of other safety measures. At any rate, adding a good pair of auxiliary or "fog lights" can significantly increase a rider's cone of vision, and installing aftermarket LED tail marker lights provides more warning to vehicles approaching from the rear.

Somehow, when driving at night, destinations can seem more distant, but eventually I rolled up the driveway, killed the engine, and swung down the sidestand, ending one more nocturnal adventure. Truth be told, I enjoyed the ride and would do it again, but for most of my time on the bike, I'll make that John Mayer line my motto: "Keep me where the light is."

36
JUST SAYING NO . . .
TO WINTER!

In January and February, weekends in the upper Midwest are often a problem for me. I can only watch rehashes of the last NFL season, clean my basement, or binge-watch myself through old seasons of *24* so many times before I have to get out and do something. My knees are shot, so cross country skiing would probably put me in a wheelchair. Snowshoeing, though I can appreciate the aesthetic attraction, combines two of my least favorite activities, hard labor and a glacial rate of speed, and I will forever be mystified over why someone would want to spend an afternoon doing something called "curling." So, I was basically up for anything when Editor Bill Wiegand asked me if I'd be interested in watching some motorcycle ice racing.

On a Sunday in late January, I gathered my riding buddy Ralph for a road trip to a nearby lake, where an official Central Wisconsin Ice Racing Association (CWIRA) event was scheduled. After a drive giving us enough time to dispose of the most important topics of the day (BMW's new G 310, why no one merges correctly anymore, and yoga pants), we threaded our way through a campground to a parking area next to Partridge Lake in Fremont, Wisconsin. I was immediately greeted by Jim Falke, president of the CWIRA for the last ten years, who was more than happy to show me around, introduce me to some of the racers, and give me some background about the sport.

Jim, who's been an ice racer both on two and four wheels for more than twenty years said, "You know, it's just a lot of fun; you get caught up in it. Normally the weather is good in the winter for ice racing—usually twenty to thirty degrees is wonderful—it's just an enjoyable day."

Jim pointed out some of the differences in the bikes used for ice racing, most obviously the tires. Most riders at this race were using tires professionally studded by Larry Strangfele. Called "Strange Tires," they have strategically placed studs turned in different directions for the best traction. Ice racing bikes are also required to have modified fenders, parallel to the ground with the leading edge perpendicular to keep the wicked-looking studs away from riders racing in packs as tight as any I've seen at Road America.

Without the "wrapped" fenders, Jim felt that ice racing could be more dangerous than enduro or motocross in the summer. One rider, Mark Muth from Black River Falls who's been involved in ice racing for forty years, showed me scars crisscrossing the top of one hand resulting from tipping down in front of another bike before the special fenders were required. Another rider that day, Jack Potter from Tomah, said he thought ice racing was actually less dangerous than summer motocross or enduro, since normally ice racing tracks are level and generally have even traction throughout.

Riders tear down straightaways, often at more than eighty miles an hour, and lean through turns with one foot out, much like flat track dirt racers. "Racing on the ice, the set-up of the bike is more important than anything else," Jim claimed. "Also, you can have a lot of power and be a good rider, but if you can't transfer your skills to the ice, which is obviously slipperier than sand, mud, or dirt, then you're not going to do well."

Hondas seemed to be king at this ice race (mostly 650s, 450s, and 250s) though there were a few Husqvarna, Yamaha, Suzuki, and KTM bikes around. Riders told me they wear basically all the protection one would use for racing in the dirt, especially knee and elbow pads, and often more because of the cold temps. Races are usually held on lakes; however, sometimes the half-mile tracks are created on flooded fairground spaces. The event had all the feel of a rally, with friends swapping stories in each other's heated trailers, food vendors grilling up brats and burgers, and family groups watching tiny riders earning their stripes in Junior Motorcycle Classes and on Peewee Quads.

One racer, Joe Haasl from Wisconsin Rapids, was trying ice racing for the first time because he "just wanted to get out and ride." A dirt racer during the summer who had been practicing on his own, he said, "You've got to learn to get forward, pitch the bike sideways, and get on the throttle early." Christian Johnson, a racer who had turned pro a few years earlier, told me, like many of the riders I spoke with, he had started racing before he reached his teens. Both a dirt and ice racer, Christian said he felt more confident on the ice because he could hold the bike wide open on the consistent surface. A summer and winter pro rider for more than ten years, Brian Franzen from Edgar had formerly raced snowmobiles. "This is just for fun," he said. "You don't win anything; you try racing for money, you'll go broke." When I mentioned I didn't figure on seeing any BMWs, he said. "Bring one out, we'll ride anything!"

Once the races started, the air was filled with cheers from fans and the roar of red-lined engines. I didn't see any racers slide out, despite ferocious speeds on the straights and elbow-to-elbow jostling through the right- and left-handers. Who won or lost seemed to be less of a concern to both riders and fans than simply sharing this triumph of preparation, skill, and spirit over the trials of another, long Midwest winter. Conditions began to deteriorate as Ralph and I watched, with the weather oscillating between rain and sleet, but it didn't seem to affect the enthusiasm of the fans or racers.

Looking for something to cure the winter blues in snow country? Next winter, I prescribe the bikes, brats, friendly family atmosphere, and racing excitement waiting for you at your nearest ice racing association event!

37
Mayday Moments

When I was in fourth or fifth grade, my pal, Steve, and I would make a monthly pilgrimage on our Schwinns out to the edge of town to a resale shop called Kruetzer's. The place was dark and gloomy, and a permanent haze of cigarette smoke emanated from a grumpy, gray-haired clerk in the back who perched on a barstool, chain smoking his way through crossword puzzles. Thick grey dust layered practically all the "merchandise" which could include anything from an old catcher's mitt left out in the rain one too many times to a disassembled tube radio to a crusted portable cement mixer. But back in one corner in a battered cardboard box was our destination, a sprawling pile of used comic books.

Comics were five for a quarter at Kruetzer's, and sitting crossed-legged on the grimy floor, we would solemnly sort through the mess, building our piles of keepers. As comic connoisseurs, we cast aside anything as puerile as an *Archie and Jughead* or a *Richie Rich*, searching for the hard stuff—war comics. Invariably there'd be a panel in one of those where a grizzled pilot of a Japanese Zero sneered through his windscreen and strafed the wings of an American Mustang piloted by a hard-faced guy with a name like Buck Skyrider (AKA-AKA-AKA-AKA-AK). Our hero Buck, with blood trickling down his forehead and smoke pouring into his cockpit, would be screaming into his mic, "SKYRIDER TO BASE! I'M HIT, I'M HIT, HAVE TO DITCH! MAYDAY! MAYDAY!"

I always wondered why "Mayday" would be used as a call of distress. May to me suggested little girls fashioning garlands of dandelions into delicate head bands and skipping around a gaily ribbon-ed maypole. It wasn't until just recently that I read somewhere that "Mayday" is actually a misnomer. The expression comes from the French "*M'aidez*" (Help Me), which makes a heck of lot more sense.

However you spell it, anyone who's spent some time on a bike has probably had his or her share of "Mayday Moments." I guess my first came when I was young and stupid(-er). An archetypal hippie, I had a full beard at the time, and I hated the way my helmet's chinstrap matted it down, so of course, I never buckled it. Though I cultivated the look of a champion of the counterculture, come to think of it, I was hopelessly vain. Anyway, as I made a right turn at an intersection, I hit some fine sand and did a slow lowside. Apart from a bruised ego and torn jeans, I was unhurt, but my Honda was lying on its side in the street, and my helmet had instantaneously popped off my head and tumbled to the opposite curb. A motorist in a suit and tie stopped and helped me right the bike and get going, politely avoiding any comment concerning the considerable role luck may have played in preventing my brains from being strewn across the pavement.

Another Mayday Moment occurred a few years ago when I had taken my R 1150 R out into the sticks trout fishing. After a fruitless few hours spent wading the Little Wolf, I packed up my gear and headed out of the parking area and up a steeply-pitched gravel ramp. Near the top the roadster slewed sideways as the rear wheel began to spin, and though I was in near-panic mode at the thought of dumping the heavy bike on this steep incline in the middle of nowhere, for once I actually did the right thing and got on the throttle, squirting me up onto the blacktop. Cue the enormous sigh of relief.

My most recent Mayday Moment occurred at a busy intersection where I waited, first in line, for the light to change to enter a four-lane expressway. When I got the green, I began to enter the intersection, but suddenly caught a silver blur approaching from my left. The blur became a full-sized silver SUV running the red light at about fifty miles per hour. I squeezed and jumped on the brakes, and the SUV's bumper passed within inches of my front wheel. Stunned, I sat there for a moment, then looked up to see the drivers of all the cars now stopped at the intersection shaking their heads in disbelief.

Mayday moments come with the territory when you're a motorcyclist, and as I look back on mine, I can see a pattern. It seems like the younger and less experienced I was, the more frequent were those white knuckle moments. But time spent on the road isn't the only factor that has reduced my Mayday quotient. I owe a lot to the words of experts like David Hough (sadly, now retiring), Fred Rau, Lee Parks, and Ken Condon. Rally workshops, "tune-up" courses, and videos have been helpful too. To borrow a phrase from Matt Parkhouse, "Always learning, always learning."

38

THE BAREST ESSENTIALS

I've found you meet the nicest people—no, not on a Honda—at the dog park. Where I take my lab Penny Lane, the usual routine is to walk a path around the five-acre field while your mutt runs, jumps, humps, and plays keepaway with whatever ill-sorted mob of pooches that happen to be around. Often I wind up walking with two or three owners I've never met before, and I've discovered that just may be the last refuge of stimulating conversation. The dogs provide an instant bond to break the ice, and few owners choose to risk getting trampled while engrossed in a cell phone.

Anyway, a few days ago a young man with a labradoodle did a few laps with me and Penny, and when it was revealed I am a moto-journalist, he started peppering me with questions about riding. His re-enlistment bonus was burning a hole in his pocket, and he was thinking motorcycle. My usual response to prospective riders is to be solemnly neutral. I'm torn between offering support and telling sobering cautionary tales. Once we got past my gruesome fatality stats and my recommendations on what kind of bike he should get (start small!), he wanted to know my recommendations for bare essentials he'd need beyond the bike itself. Pretty much in order of importance, this is basically what I told him:

1. Helmet: I've had the opportunity to test a lot of helmets, and though I have favorite brands, my seasoned opinion is not surprising: you get what you pay for. There is more than one difference between a $100 and a $400 helmet; the question is, "What's your brain worth to you?" My personal preference for the kind of riding I do most of the time (street, some touring) is a quality flip-up, and though first models were pretty clunky, the newest have come a long way toward offering the same comfort and safety as full-faced lids.

2. Jacket and Pants: I should say two jackets. Though there are definitely some ingenious efforts to produce a true, three-season jacket suite, I have gravitated to a ballistic mesh jacket with elbow, shoulder, and back armor for the summer, and an armored, single-layer textile jacket for everything else. I usually wear textile, single layer pants with hip and knee armor, but I've also dabbled with clever protective jeans and pants that can pass for casual wear. I've tried riding suits, and I think they're great, but again, for the kind of short-hop riding that I mostly do, I'm more comfortable in a two-piece (riding ensemble!), using layers to adjust to the weather.

3. Gloves: A year or so ago I slipped my hands into a pair of Fly heated gloves. Along with heated grips and handguards, my hands, what T.S. Eliot would call "ragged claws," are living the dream come October/November. In warmer months I'm usually wearing elkskin. As a testament for my version of handwriting , my kids once spent weeks before Christmas looking for gloves made of *elf*skin! No luck.

4. Ear Plugs: Twisted Throttle sells "No Noise" ear protection. These plugs were developed for Dutch police to

specifically screen out wind blast, but still allow you to hear sirens and conversation. They do that pretty well, but I'm notorious for forgetting which pocket I've tucked them into. My failsafe solution is a bottle of thirty-two decibel foam plugs I find in Walmart's hunting department.

5.   Kickstand Foot: I'm lucky to have a son who runs a metal fabrication plant, so I usually (with his help) make my own permanently attached kickstand foot every time I switch bikes, since finding one that nests properly when retracted yet has a big enough footprint is often a trial and error experience (and I'm cheap). You can carry kickstand plates in your tank bag (Aerostich has a CARBON FIBER model!) but I think every one I've purchased or made myself has sadly been left behind as I've lackadaisically driven off into the sunset. Incidentally, there's never an empty can around when you need one.

6.   Windshield: Okay, okay, some will say I'm a wimp—real riders don't need a windshield. But I have ridden in rain storms—heck, I've ridden in snow storms—and going without a real windshield (not the GS's standard shield) is a part of the "adventure" I can do without.

7.   Top Case: In my own crude, mechanically disinclined way I've bolted a top case to every bike I've owned and never regretted it. (Well, there was that one time when a female acquaintance caught her foot on the case while mounting up and fell over the bike.) My all-time favorite is a Pelican 1500. I've seen Pelicans blasted with buckshot, run over by trucks, and pitched into the ocean with no loss of integrity. They're padlocking secure, positive latching tight, and O-ring sealing waterproof. They even have purge valves for changes in air pressure!

8.   Auxiliary Lights: My present GS has a pair of Clearwater Lights Darla driving lights mounted low on my crash bars in an attempt to create the famous conspicuity triangle. These lights are adjustable in intensity and can be set up to go to full power when you switch to brights. You can

order them with amber covers, which I feel makes me even more noticeable.

9.   De-accelerometer Tail Lights: What started with a couple guys tinkering in garages has turned into a slew of products on the market, all offering the same safety feature: bright LEDs that blink to signal de-acceleration with or without riders touching their brakes. If you don't know about these, you should. I predict one day they will come as standard equipment on all street bikes.

10.   Throttle Lock: The ragged claws thing again. Having spent a good share of my life stroking a Vic Firth 7A drumstick, my right grip doesn't last long on an extended highway run. Along with a Crampbuster grip lever, I've used a few types of mechanical throttle locks so far, my favorites being those that click off the moment the front brake lever is squeezed, and though it's true they don't maintain a constant speed on hills or in the wind like a true cruise control would, with my mechanical ineptitude and parsimonious nature, they've been a godsend.

That's a long list, but I could see my new dog park friend was still bike bound, though recalculating how to allocate his bonus check. Of course, I didn't mention the obvious number one essential piece of equipment, since he's a millennial: a cell phone.

39
THE BAREST ESSENTIALS,
PART DEUX

In the April issue of *BMW Owners News*, I satisfied my editor's insatiable demand for another column at least as long as one by K-bike idolater Jack Riepe by musing about what kinds of add-ons, accessories, and gear were more than just sparkly baubles but were actually essentials in terms of safety, comfort, and convenience. I limited myself to ten, but invited my faithful readers to share their additions to my list.

Dr. Dan Perkins, who has retired from riding but still wears his fifteen-year MOA pin proudly, showed me (in fact graciously *gave* me) a pair of what I'd guess you'd call motorcycle gaiters. Much like those lobster claw over-gloves riders carry to keep their gloves dry and rain from crawling up under their jacket sleeves, these nylon gaiter thing-ys cup the toes of your boots and extend up nearly to your knee, with elastic at the top. Dan claimed that as long as he had the foresight to pull these on before the heavens opened up, he'd never had wet boots or pant legs. He added that the BMW MOA's *Anonymous Book* should be considered an essential for all members. On a trip years ago to Vancouver, Dan recounted how he and a buddy called up a number there from the book, and though the member was at college, he had left instructions with his mother to welcome anyone who called. They were treated to three days of free room and board!

In a similar vein, Robert Stickland told me he'd insert a good pair of boots right behind my #3, gloves. A reader after my own heart since he also rides an F 700 GS (albeit in the white and red scheme I covet), Robert says he never touches his bike without wearing a helmet, boots, and gloves.

David Stroud from Northern Virginia agreed with my #1, a decent helmet, and told me he has two crashed helmets that did their job, ready to show anyone who needs convincing. On his bike, David always carries a custom tool kit, at least holding enough equipment to repair a flat and do a 6K maintenance, and a small flashlight. Since he's had to repair two flats in ninety-seven degree heat, he also suggests always carrying a liter of water, or even more to help with finding a puncture. Having served his country on several continents, David likes to carry some emergency first aid supplies, recommending an Israeli bandage, two tourniquets (one is none), a small rag or two, a small roll of leukotape-P , a small bottle of crazy glue (for cuts), and some waterproof band-aids.

When wearing his Aerostich Roadcrafter in the summer, Kerry Burrage wrote he likes to soak a T-shirt and bandana at rest stops. He claims it keeps him cool as a cucumber, though he often gets a few strange looks. He recalled someone outside a Seven Eleven once asked him if his 'stich had air conditioning. He replied, "Yes sir, yes it does."

More than one member also suggested I should have listed a cell phone, cash, and a credit card in my top five, while others told me they're married to their GPS units and SPOT trackers.

When it comes to touring, some mentioned a good cycle cover can come in mighty handy, in more ways than one.

I'd say these are all great suggestions when it comes to "barest essentials," moreover hearing these comments made me consider one more time how valuable it is to be a member of associations like the BMW MOA with the portal it opens to so many miles of shared experience.

40
"RALLY VIRGIN"

Since I write and edit for a motorcycle magazine, and of course, I own a motorcycle, people may tend to assume I'm some kind of expert about bikes and riding them. Well, I'm not. Sure, I've owned a bunch of bikes (the last four Beemers), and have taken a few road trips, but I'm more what some might call an "enthusiast." And years ago, when I had just joined the MOA, I was even more of a tenderfoot. Because of that, I was a little intimidated by the prospect of attending my first big gathering, the BMW MOA International Rally, and I had little idea of what to expect.

As my riding buddy Ralph and I drew closer to the rally site that year, I remember seeing more and more bikes funneling onto the interstate we were on, all headed in the same direction. Head nods, friendly waves, and the occasional horn toot marked almost every encounter. This was really my first hint as to what kind of community I had joined.

When we parked outside the rally to register, I gaped, wide-eyed, at the long line of motorcycles (mostly BMWs) and the queue of all kinds of cyclists in all kinds of gear, no clue that this would be nothing compared to the masses of bikes and riders inside the rally grounds.

After filling out my paperwork and handing it in to a friendly volunteer, he skimmed it quickly and shouted, "RALLY VIRGIN!" Almost everyone in the tent turned in our direction and clapped, whistled, and hooted. I'm not sure if that's still always done or if everyone thinks it's particularly appropriate, but for me, it felt like good-natured ribbing, the kind you get from your family.

Once done registering, loading up my swag (coffee cup, backsack, patch, and pin), and setting up camp in the middle of a growing sea of tents and bikes, I headed for the vendor area. Since I was then just beginning to write gear reviews (and am a self-avowed farkle-holic), the siren song of the vendor booths was impossible to resist. As I was fondling a helmet at one booth, a company rep approached, greeted me, pointed out some features of the lid in my hands, and then asked, "So what kind of helmet are you using now?" When I mentioned the brand of the eBay special I was using, he smirked, "That's no helmet." I was a little piqued at first, but after he patiently schooled me on all the finer points of helmet history, design, and construction, I went to the Cybercafé and ordered a new one online immediately.

The workshops were also packed with good information. For instance, one airhead savant joked about the perils of using zipties (which represent the pinnacle of my mechanical expertise), his buddy noting he had recently needed five stitches for using them without a special ziptie gun—my reaction: A what? The atmosphere of all the workshops I attended was informal but informative, the tone more of sharing than sermonizing, and I think even newbies like me felt comfortable asking any kind of question, no matter how elementary.

That night, I gravitated to the mainstage area, where the music began with Bavarian oom-pah music, followed by some good classic rock. New friends were made, the dark beer, kettle corn, and conversation ebbed and flowed, and I ended up sitting in rapt awe as a fellow member recounted the miles he had traveled and worldwide waypoints he had touched. It made me feel a little like a poser, but my catagelophobia (the fear of being ridiculed) vanished, as he confessed he liked nothing more than prowling back roads just a few miles from his home on a beat-up K-bike.

By the last day of my first rally all my apprehensions were gone. I sat on a bench and met a woman who had ridden hundreds of miles with her husband and two little dogs. I met another rider who was looking forward to a workshop on tires, before he chose which brand to have spooned on right at the rally before he headed back to Boston. I watched a GS demo, which I could enjoy without questioning my own skill. I marveled at the pristine look of the bikes at the Vintage Display corral. I had one of the best fish fries (al fresco) of my life (and having grown up in Wisconsin, that's saying a lot).

I packed up the next morning, snicked into first gear, and eased out of the rally grounds, happy to be on the road again but regretting the rally was over.

Whether it's the BMW MOA International Rally, the RA National, the Wing Ding, Americade, Daytona Bike Week, Laconia, Myrtle Beach, or Sturgis, there are a few things I've come to expect from any place where riders gather: fun, fellowship, new-found knowledge, and best of all, the pervasive atmosphere of community.

41

Re-Discovering the Heart
of the Driftless Area

*All paths are the same, leading nowhere. Therefore,
pick a path with heart! –Carlos Castaneda*

Like many of my baby boomer brethren, most of my efforts
during my college days seemed devoted to anything but
preparing myself for the world of work. I was free to dabble in
all kinds of alternative activities and philosophies and spent
some time pouring through Carlos Castaneda's then popular
novels. Dog-eared copies of books like *The Teachings of Don
Juan*, *A Separate Reality*, and *Journey to Ixtlan* were poking
out of a lot of backpacks in the early '70s, and though I was
intrigued with them then, about the only thing that stuck
with me was the idea of a "power spot." According to Don
Juan, the "Man of Knowledge" in the novels, everyone has
a power spot, unique to him or her, and once discovered, it
affords a rejuvenation of energy and clarity of vision.

The highlight of my spring semesters back then was
escaping the college grind to spend weekends on my sister's

farm down in the heart of southwest Wisconsin's Driftless Area. I'd spend foggy mornings down in the hollows, wading one of the countless, cool-running spring creeks to pluck out a few brown trout and some fresh watercress, and later I'd hike (more like "climb") into the lush, near vertically-sloped coulees searching for morel mushrooms. I remember thinking this just might be my own power spot. Once I had scraped up enough cash for a used, red and white Honda CB350 and began spending afternoons threading my way through the squiggly state, county, and township roads, this new dimension confirmed the mystic power Wisconsin's so-called "Coulee Country" held for me.

So last spring when Editor Bill Wiegand asked me to spend a few days poking around this same area as an advance man for a scheduled "Weekend Getaway" in the Driftless Area, I couldn't load my panniers fast enough.

My first day out, I headed directly to Black River Falls, site of a fall "Getaway." Black River Falls sits near the northeast reaches of the strip of southwest Wisconsin known as the Driftless Area. It's called "Driftless" since it escaped getting mowed down and covered in "drift" by the last glacier, though as the glacier receded, its meltwater carved this area of Wisconsin into a maze of deep valleys, steep coulees, and bluffs. This kind of topography has made southwest Wisconsin legendary for motorcyclists seeking endless roller coasters of pavement through spectacular scenery. I made a stop at the award-winning Sand Creek Brewing Company, Wisconsin's third largest craft beer brewery, but not feeling especially lucky, I passed on stopping in to roll the dice or pull the handles on a few one-armed bandits at the popular Ho-Chunk Gaming Black River Falls, which also offers accommodations.

Just southwest of Black River Falls is Wisconsin's "Cranberry Country." Something like 120 thousand visitors will converge for a weekend every summer on little Warrens, Wisconsin, for the "Cranberry Festival," a three-day gathering for food, music, parades, and over 1,000 craft, food, and flea market vendors. Those curious about the cranberry culture of Wisconsin can visit the Cranberry Discovery Center in Warrens, open Monday through Sunday, 9AM to 5PM.

Just a ways east out of Black River Falls on Highway 54 is North Settlement Road, one of Wisconsin's "Rustic Roads." Heading south, it meanders for about twelve miles through the Black River State Forest's pine plantations, marshes, and hardwood stands, which are a palette of vibrant colors in the fall. The road was not in the best shape when I traveled it, with occasional potholes and patches of gravel where culverts had been replaced, but riders are bound to see a variety of wildlife and diverse plant life, including sphagnum peat moss beds and native wildflowers.

North Settlement Road ends at County O, and from there, the quickest route to the most popular Driftless Area roads is to take County O west to State Highway 27 south. Highway 27 passes through Sparta, where tourers may want to take a break at the Deke Slayton Memorial Space and Bicycle Museum. Slayton, one of our first astronauts, was a member of the Mercury 7 group and part of the crew for the US/Russian Apollo-Soyuz docking mission. The bicycle part of the museum has over eighty two-wheelers that span centuries of history. Sparta lays claim to being "the bicycling capital of America" and is the trail head for one of the first "Rails to Trails" programs, the Elroy-Sparta Bike Trail. Called "the Granddaddy of them all," the Elroy-Sparta Trail covers thirty-two miles through rolling countryside and three tunnels, one of them three-quarters of a mile long (shuttles and bike rentals are available at both ends of the trail). There is also an aviation section of the museum that features dozens of model planes, including a model of the Wright brothers' first plane and a full-size 1932 Pietenpol.

Continue south on Highway 27 to Cashton, pick up Highway 33, and you're in for some of the most memorable rides of your life. Taking Highway 33 east for a few miles will lead you to Wisconsin's answer to "The Tail of the Dragon," up and over Wildcat Mountain. Just for the fun of it, I like to turn around and head right back over the mountain and back to Ontario, then turn south on Highway

131, a favorite of many riders for its pleasant sweepers and gorgeous scenery.

Highway 131 cuts through the Kickapoo Valley Reserve, 8,569 acres of sandstone cliffs and forested bluffs towering over the sweeping valleys cradling the Kickapoo River. Recognized as a National Natural Landmark, a State Natural Area, and prime wetland habitat for birds and other wildlife, the Reserve also has a fascinating history. Back in the '60s, in response to periodic flooding problems (probably due in some part to logging and farming activities), a congress-initiated program called for the river to be dammed with the idea of creating a recreational resource and sparing downstream communities from flooding. Over 140 families sold or were forced to sell their homes and businesses. Construction began, but soon budget and environmental concerns halted the project, and though some huge concrete structures eerily still rise from the valley, most of the Reserve has returned to its natural state. A visitor's center for the Kickapoo Valley Reserve is open 8AM to 4:30PM, Monday through Saturday.

Just before leaving the reserve heading south, on the advice of a local rider, I took a left on County P. This little stretch from 131 over to Highway 82 will give you all the twisties you could ever want. As you round one of the countless bends bordered by rocky outcroppings, you may feel as if you've ridden suddenly into the 1800s. Working Amish farms, small bakeries, produce and wood working shops, and quaint cabins speckle this area, but keep an eye out for buggies and, of course, the occasional horse manure deposit!

If you skip County P, leaving the Reserve on south 131, you'll pass Wildthings Fur Company, where I couldn't resist picking up some locally-caught smoked trout. You can watch hats, caps, mittens, and motorcycle seat covers being made from everything from wolverine to wolf fur, and I decided to get my saddle sized for a sheepskin pad. A block down the highway is the "ALMOST world famous" Rockton Bar, where its renowned chicken barbecue packs its parking lot each Sunday with both two-wheeled and four-footed transportation (there are many equestrians in this area).

Another Rustic Road in the area I'd recommend meets Highway 131 just as you leave the Reserve to the south. The Rustic Roads sign there clearly marks its beginning at Dutch

Hollow Road, but watch the signs carefully, as Dutch Hollow magically turns into Sand Hill Road. Turn right at Lower Ridge Road, which will lead you back to Highways 131 and 33 and into Ontario, which is proclaimed by its welcome sign to be "The Canoeing Capital of the World." This side tour has some great elevations providing scenic overlooks and threads its way past Amish farms and horse stables.

Located to the west on Highway 82 is Hillsboro, a common rallying point for groups riding the Driftless Area. The Hillsboro Brewing Company (first established in 1846) in the middle of town offers a scrumptious and varied menu (try the nachos!) and craft beers from their brewery just down the street. As testament to the popularity of the area for motorcyclists, just outside of Hillsboro is the Blue Highway Motorcycle Lodge. The six, elegantly crafted cabins there are only available to motorcyclists, and though they are situated on forty secluded acres of a forested bluff, each cabin boasts four-star accommodations. The night I was lucky to stay there I was pleasantly surprised by all the special touches owners Dan and Brandy have included at each cabin. Besides the paved paths leading to each cabin, fresh fruit, whirlpool tubs, boot dryers, gas fireplaces, kitchenettes, screened porches, and even motorcycle-ports to keep bikes out of the elements make this stop tailor-made for riders.

After another day crisscrossing the area, I stayed for a night at the Blakely Hobbit (*page 198*) near Viola (home to the internationally known S&S Cycle; call ahead for tours). It's been said you can't turn around in the Driftless Area without stepping into a trout stream, and the Hobbit cabins overlook one of the most famous of these, the West Fork of the Kickapoo River. Like many bed and breakfasts and cabins in the area catering to anglers, the Hobbit may be a little rustic for some; however, the unspoiled views, the quiet serenity, and the personal attention from Eddi, the owner for over thirty years, made this a great, restful spot for me. The Hobbit offers two cabins, tent camping, and RV parking, all on the banks of the gently burbling West Fork.

Heading south on State Highway 82/56 led me to Viroqua, a small town with a large number of unique attractions. The Saturday Farm Market features many booths offering locally grown, organic produce, Amish baked goods, pastured meats, and preserves, as well as handmade crafts and furniture. Visitors also enjoy taking the walking or driving tours of local vineyards and the unique round barns that dot the area. Other unique attractions include the Fourtney Underground Theater and the Viroqua Food Cooperative, which serves three meals a day made from local and organic foods and is popular for its soup and salad bar. I can vouch for their paninis!

From Viroqua, it's a short run west on State Highway 14 to the Mississippi, the western boundary of the Wisconsin portion of the Driftless Area, and Highway 35, "The Great River Road." This route, traveling both north and south, is nationally known by motorcyclists for its majestic views of the Mississippi river and the bluffs that bracket it, especially in the fall when colors peak and clouds of migrating wildfowl use this flyway. Visitors in late fall should check the dates of La Crosse's Octoberfest, since traffic around then can get pretty heavy. Depending on how you feel about crowds, Octoberfest features three days of fun activities, including parades, music, a craft beer night, countless food vendors, contests, and as much lederhosen as you'd ever care to see.

Northeast of La Crosse, many riders make a pilgrimage of sorts to the Mindoro Cut. At the summit of a cavalcade of twisties and switchbacks, County Trunk C (formerly State Highway 108) slashes down through 74 feet of solid dolomite and sandstone, earning it the title as the second deepest hand-hewn cut in the Western Hemisphere and a place on the National Register of Historic Places. Visitors can pick up County C north in West Salem, just east of La Crosse, and after traversing the cut, motorcyclists are often drawn to Top Dawgs Pub and Grub in Mindoro. Though it might look a little shabby from the outside, Top Dawgs is known for offering 108 different hamburgers, not to mention locally made, fresh bleu cheese "to die for." Each time you sample one of the burgers, your ticket is punched, and after trying the full menu you earn a free steak dinner. Paul, the owner, told me Top Dawgs has served riders from all over the world, and get this, he claims he opens at 4:30AM and closes the place sometimes as late as 2AM!

It's impossible to do more than just scratch the surface of riding and touring opportunities in southwestern Wisconsin; in fact, once you're in the Driftless Area, it's a challenge to find a route you won't enjoy. However, remember much of this area is rural, and this means deer, buggies, bicyclists, and a bunch more things to stay alert for. Coming around one sweeper near Hillsboro, I was even confronted with a recalcitrant cow, and another rider told me she had just had a face-off with a donkey. So, take your time, and enjoy this wonderful resource of motorcycling adventure. In addition to the links below, many of the routes I've mentioned can be viewed on YouTube, but for a comprehensive look at maps of six suggested motor routes and eighty-eight attractions, visit DriftlessDestinations.com or pick up one of their free brochures available at restaurants, hotels, and convenience stores in the area.

Whether or not the southwestern Wisconsin Driftless Area becomes your "power spot," as it has for me, its exciting roads are what Castaneda might have called "paths with heart," and if I can borrow one more quote from him, " . . . there I travel looking, looking breathlessly."

Links to more information:
Black River Falls Getaway Information: www.bmwmoa. org/ (select "Events," "MOA Getaway Black River Falls")
Sand Creek Brewing: sandcreekbrewing.com/
Ho-Chunk Gaming Black River Falls: ho-chunkgaming. com/blackriverfalls/
Cranberry Discovery Center: discovercranberries.com/

Deke Slayton Space and Bicycle Museum: dekeslaytonmuseum.org/

Kickapoo Valley Reserve: kickapoovalley.wi.gov/Home

Wildthings Fur Company: wildthingsfur.com/

Blue Highway Motorcycle Lodge: bluehighwaymotorcyclelodge.net/

The Blakley Hobbit: blakleyhobbit.com/

S&S Cycle: www.sscycle.com/

La Crosse Octoberfest: oktoberfestusa.com/

Viroqua Tourism: viroqua-wisconsin.com/viroqua-tourism/what-to-do/area-attractions

Driftless Destinations: driftlessdestinations.com

42
ON THE TRAIL OF
"THE GRAND ADVENTURE"

I'm a baby. At least that's what my wife says, and she's been saying that more and more frequently every time I start complaining about my advancing age, my accumulating aches and pains, and the consequent medical appointments and procedures. I've also been reading the features and letters in moto-magazines and hearing comments from other riders at rallies that offer varying responses to the reality of getting up in years, staying healthy, and the decisions it drives. Rather than viewing growing older and becoming a "vintage motorcyclist" as what my wife calls "The Grand Adventure," I've become more inclined to dread it as an ever-expanding cavalcade of new restrictions and humiliations, exponentially growing in frequency and degree, one of which is changing your riding habits, and another is the periodic colonoscopy, having a stranger probe your innermost sanctums. But apparently it's now some kind of AMA cosmic law that says everybody must include this procedure into their descent into decrepitude, so who am I to question that?

The experience began with dutifully following the first of five pages of written directions to purchase a gallon of Gatorade (your choice of flavor) and a powder which I have now surmised was derived from a particularly toxic uranium isotope. Mixed together, the cocktail is designed to "cleanse your gastrointestinal system." It does that. In fact, after it had done its work, I felt as if the only thing left inside my skin was my skeleton. You're also instructed to not eat anything, a rule not hard to follow, since I figured even tea and toast would drop through me like a cabbage down a chimney.

At the hospital my wife insulated herself from my sarcasms, petulant questions, and general whining with a *People* magazine,(yes, you have to take someone along to witness your ordeal and share all the amusing details of your cowardly behavior later with all acquaintances, the grocery checkout clerk, and anyone else in a four-mile radius). I stripped (the process all institutions use to reduce you to a bowl of quivering Jello) and donned the sheet of recycled paper generously known as a gown, the backside conveniently left open for the coming invasion.

A parade of cheery nurses came through my curtained off cubicle, repeatedly making sure I was who I said I was and exchanging gossip, commiserating tales of childbirth, and empathetic eye rolls with my wife. It took me back to when I was a little boy being forced to try on pants with my mom and the clerk chuckling behind me in a three-pane mirror.

I was given the choice of two drugs: Benzodiazepin and Propofol, the latter being billed as, "You know, the stuff they gave Michael Jackson." Having had the first before with real problems coming back to earth, and because I've always liked *The Man in the Mirror*, I opted for the Propofol.

Finally, it was time to wheel my cart, or "guernsey" or whatever you call it, into the subzero "Procedure Room," full of a starship array of diagnostic screens and equipment that made a BMW service bay look like Edison's workshop. The doctor proudly displayed the six-foot black snake which would soon be slithering up my most private areas, positively beaming while he explained what an entertaining experience this would be for all. I thought, "Can we please start the drugs now?" A young lady then came in and busied herself booting up the computers and monitors, once again confirming they had trapped the correct victim. She then turned to me, and her face suddenly brightened.

"MR. DAVIS!!! IT'S ME!"

Oh God, please tell me the drugs are already working.

"MR. DAVIS!!! DO YOU REMEMBER ME? I WAS IN YOUR HIGH SCHOOL PHOTOGRAPHY CLASS!!! DOCTOR, HE WAS MY FAVORITE HIGH SCHOOL TEACHER!"

I frantically scanned for the anesthetic IV; could I insert it myself?

Having no recollection of the young woman, I resorted to my usual technique I use when I don't recognize a former student: "Oh, you . . . "

"IT'S ME, SHANA, REMEMBER? AND LOOK, MR. DAVIS, I'M USING MY PHOTOGRAPHY SKILLS!"

The doctor and Shana together pointed to a four by five foot monitor hovering over my torso. My doctor grinned and said, "Shana here will be monitoring all phases of your colonoscopy."

Please God, I was promised drugs.

"That's great, um, Shana; it's been a while . . . "

My prodigal student then launched into a lengthy recitation of all her vital career statistics, how many children she had, when she was in my class, what had become of the most prominent members of her class, and how many of them would be happy to hear of our star-crossed reunion on her Facebook page.

Finally, mercifully, they put me out. The next thing I knew I was back in my curtained cloister, my wife absorbed in a story about a new Kardashian milestone.

Now, don't get me wrong. Getting a colonoscopy, starting at age fifty and repeating every ten years is obviously a great idea. I've read that seventy-five to ninety percent of colon cancer cases can be prevented through colonoscopy screening, in addition to helping diagnose other intestinal problems. And my wife is probably right, I can be kind of a baby, or on the other hand, a cantankerous old curmudgeon. And unless you too have served as a teacher for six or seven thousand students over your career, you probably won't have to suffer the kind of experience I had. But would I term this part of "The Grand Adventure?" No.

As I was preparing to leave, a positively ebullient nurse said, "If your test looks good, you don't have to do this again for ten years, and then, you'll probably only need to bring in a stool sample!" Ah, something to look forward to: ten years into my Grand Adventure I'll be on equal footing with my Labrador Retriever.

Experiences like these make it hard to avoid thinking about the diminishing number of years I may be able to keep saddling up on my bike and heading for parts unknown. Yes, I can be a baby about it, but instead, it's probably better to focus on appreciating how lucky I am to be able to ride each new, beckoning mile.

43
THINK SMALL

Like probably a lot of riders around my age, I once went through a riding sabbatical. For some, it might have been for financial reasons or possibly there were young ones in the house that made risk-taking seem less than prudent, discretion being the better part of valor. In my case, it was both.

I had ridden bikes right up to the point my son was born and had covered enough miles and seen enough accidents, even involving close friends, to know how easily a ride could suddenly go south. I had taken a teaching job in a small town high school where the salary was low enough to qualify us for food stamps, and my wife worked part-time nights at a farm co-op while I did child care. A motorcycle was considered by both of us a luxury and a risk, so selling the Honda 450 was not an issue.

For the next twenty years my motorcycle experience was limited to magazine subscriptions, Peter Egan books, and occasional rides on a Honda scrambler or a Triumph when friends stopped by. Though I didn't mention it (much), my wife certainly noticed my longing looks when a bike growled by, and one Christmas, with the kids finally pretty much on their own in college, she gave me a gift-wrapped, shiny black helmet—tacit approval to plunge once more into the fray.

For one of the few times in my life when I've actually let head rule over heart, I decided to start small and inexpensive. My skills, I knew, were rusty, and I had to wonder if that old passion would still be there, so best to dip a toe in rather than dive off the high board. Some browsing time on eBay eventually led me to an intriguing little 1975 Honda CB200.

According to the online description, though it was over twenty years old, the 200 had just five hundred miles on it. The owner's father originally had bought it for his wife, thinking she could join him on the road, but after a little spill on a trip around the block, she wanted nothing more to do with bikes. The Honda had then mostly sat in the garage for twenty years, gathering dust, varnishing the inside of its gas tank, gumming up its carburetors, and succumbing to a little patina of surface rust.

I couldn't remember ever hearing of a CB200, so I did a little research. The Honda 200 twin was only produced for three years, 1973 to 1976, and replaced the Honda 175. It had a few unique features, including a vinyl-topped toaster tank that made the bike look bigger than it was, dual carbs, spark plugs that fired both on the power and exhaust strokes, seventeen horses, and an ingenious cable disk brake, which you see on some bicycles today. In addition to the kickstarter, the 200 had electric start, still somewhat a novelty at the time, which made it attractive when it was in production, but it was never a huge seller, and with the public looking for something that wasn't redlined at seventy miles per hour, Honda could smell the coffee.

The bike was sitting in Hudson, Wisconsin, and armed with two thermoses of coffee and a bag of oatmeal cookies, my buddy, Ralph (who had just recently sprung for a new generation Bonny), and I set out on a bright January day to kick the tires. We had received little snow thus far that winter, so after doing a quick inspection, I could even buzz the bike up and down the driveway. It ran, I signed the cashier's check for $500, and we easily loaded the 300-pound bike into the back of my old Ford Ranger.

Once I got the bike home, Ralph and I manhandled it into the basement, where I could play with it until April. The rust was minimal, and with a thorough cleaning and polishing, the bike looked pretty spiffy. However, the tires were cracked and needed replacing, as did the battery. Determined to change the points, grease the cables, clean the carbs, and check all the fasteners and hoses, I wrestled with frozen bolts and clamps. I found the Philips-headed bolts Honda used in those days sometimes near impossible to break free, and as I pulled them, I replaced them with new, stainless hardware. One of the mufflers, as with most vintage Hondas, had begun to rot, but I was able to track down a NOS replacement on eBay. I decided to wait until I could get the bike outside to change out the oil and filter.

By March, the 200 was mechanically refreshed, and I decided to add a few niceties. I found a little smoked windscreen that fit the bike's diminutive size, and since the bike came with decent luggage rack, I added a cheap, used top case that looked a little preposterous on the back but would hold all I needed for my commutes to work. Even though the bike was light, I also added a homemade sidestand foot, something I've done for every bike I've ever owned since. Unlike many bikes today, a centerstand was standard on the CB200.

When the road finally cleared in April, I brought the bike out into the sunshine and took it for a tentative shakedown cruise. The brakes weren't anything special, but the bike didn't do anything quickly, and that was just fine for my re-entry into two-wheeled travel. The engine also coughed a bit, probably from crud still working its way out of the gas tank. I found the five-speed transmission helpful in hitting highway speed, although hills and wind meant downshifting. Really a pretty smooth ride with handling as good as could be expected.

The little 200 served me well for a year by never really allowing me to press beyond my slowly rebounding skills. Never a drop of oil, never a hard start, never a problem, and compared to the next bikes I would go through, an incredibly cheap date. I ended up selling the bike for $300 more than the purchase price and moved up to another eBay deal, a Honda 400, then caught the BMW bug. I still wax nostalgic when I browse all the new bikes in the 300-class, looking especially wistfully at that BMW G 310 GS. I heartily endorse starting small to any returning or new rider. Not only is it sensible, but it can be loads of fun as well!

44

ON ANY MONDAY

Though I'm officially retired, I haven't been able to resist taking a couple part-time jobs. One of those is at a local radio station, where like me, two of my co-workers often commute in on their motorcycles. As we unzip jackets, stow helmets and gloves, maybe shrug away a little chill, and engage in a little light-hearted banter, there's a certain energy, a certain vigor buzzing in the air. Is it my imagination that the other staff members who've arrived in cars seem sleepier, grumpier, and more resigned?

Apparently not.

A recent study completed by three researchers from UCLA indicated a healthy commute by motorcycle is a great wake-me-up. The study monitored the heart rates and brain activity of fifty riders as they rode their own bikes on a twenty-mile route. Hormone levels were also measured before, during and after the rides. Results indicated that the participants in the study "experienced an increase in adrenalin levels and heart rate as well as a decrease in metrics often associated with light exercise and stress-reduction." The study also noted a reduction in cortisol levels, a hormonal marker for stress. Heather Malenshek, Harley-Davidson's Vice President of Marketing and Brand (which, it should be noted, sponsored the study), feels the research findings support what riders have maintained for years: "There's a vitality and heightened sensory experience that comes from riding a motorcycle." (For more information, search "roadracing.com, Harley-Davidson funded study.")

Of course, my brethren in the "Commutation Nation" know choosing two wheels to get to work is not all puppies and lollipops. Sure, it can be a hassle to wrench the bike out of the garage, load the courier bag, gear up with helmet, ear plugs, boots, etcetera, and who hasn't cringed at seeing cagers drinking coffee, eating burritos, checking their email, applying make-up, or reading a newspaper as they plow past? Not to mention, each commute can offer a new collection of road hazards—was that tennis shoe in the road yesterday? That dusting of chicken feed in that shady sweeper? And anyone who commonly commutes has probably been ribbed relentlessly by co-workers all winter long—"So, ride the bike today?" Conversations with my fellow moto-commuters often begin with comments like "How'd you like that fog today?" "Chip sealin' County BB," "Skunks suck," and "Some jerk in an F-150 wouldn't get off my tail!" There's a common thread there though, one we've all noticed: though the route may be the same, every commute on a bike can be different and memorable. I have trouble remembering any particular sight, sound, smell, or feeling I've had when commuting by car.

There are also tangible benefits to commuting on a cycle, such as miles per gallon, lane splitting, less pollution, and fewer miles on the family car, but my favorite perk comes at the end of my shift at work. No matter how mind-numbing hours of staring at a computer screen, doing paperwork, or repeating the same chore ad nauseum can get, knowing my getaway bike is waiting patiently outside to join me in my escape is more rewarding than a paycheck. In my role as an editor, I don't know how many times I've read a rider's words about taking "the long way home," exploring a new country road, getting lost on purpose. Returning home, my wife sometimes asks, "What made you so late?" I answer, "My motorcycle."

I was re-reading a story the other day by Peter Egan about a motorcycle tour he and his wife took of Ireland. He wrote that, despite being dogged by drenching rain, doing the same trip by car would have been "a missed opportunity." Whether because of weather or some other reason, not using my bike to commute is an opportunity I hate to miss.

45
WORLD WIDE WONDER

Before I take that first shake-down cruise on my bike in April, it's my habit to do a little spring cleaning. I drag out the S100, the Bugslide, and the Armor All and build a small glacier of discarded shop rags, old T-shirts, and paper towels while spraying and wiping every nook and cranny I can get to. I had neglected the rear wheel for too many miles and so this spring spent at least an hour or two on that, muscling off the stubborn, tar-like coating of crud from flung chain oil. However, when I got around to the right rear side of the bike, I noticed something peculiar. As anyone who has read my past columns knows, I am no mechanic; in fact, I swear some of my metric tools hide themselves at night just so they won't have to suffer the indignities of my bumbling (especially the 10mm socket), but even in my woeful ignorance of tech, I knew that the dark molasses color of my rear brake fluid just didn't look right.

On the BMW F 700 GS, the rear brake draws fluid from a shot glass-sized reservoir just below the seat, and a quick glance at the front brake reservoir's contrasting olive oil hue confirmed my apprehension. I knew the brake fluid for the rear only had a couple thousand miles on it, so something was, indeed, hinky. Fifteen years ago, I probably would have panicked and ran to a flip phone to make an appointment at my favorite BMW dealer. But now it's 2019, and I have discovered forums. Logging in to the BMWMOA F-Twins forum, I found there has been quite a discussion about the rear brake fluid going bad in F 650s, F 700s, and F 800s. It always amazes me how esoteric forum threads can get, but that's really what makes them so cool.

The posts there, as usual, covered a wide range of tips, complaints, queries, and rants, but I've learned one has to take everything on a forum with a granule of skepticism. Unfortunately, the ability to type doesn't necessarily engender anyone with automatic expertise about motorcycles (or civility, it seems). Evidently, lots of owners had noticed this problem, but theories on its cause were varied: Cheap rubber brake lines? Excessive heat? Contamination sucked in at the caliper piston? Just sitting too long in the garage? One post claimed the contaminated fluid made the brake dangerously "squishy," while another said just forget it and follow the recommended service intervals. As many know, forum threads may start off helpful but can sometimes go south after one poster strays from the topic to personal cracks or the thread falls into the rabbit hole of which brand of fluids best be used where. But anyway, the clear majority agreed root beer-colored brake fluid was not a good thing.

More hunting on the F800riders.org forums yielded pretty much the same results, with the most commonly suggested solution being flushing. Okay, but that sounded intimidating for a guy whose mechanical know-how doesn't extend much further than "righty tighty, lefty loosey." When I had a 2004 BMW R 1150 R, with its integrated brakes, I had once considered trying a brake fluid change myself, since my local shop wanted me to spend almost three hundred dollars for the service. Skimming a shop manual revealed that, yeah, I could probably do it myself, given six months of BMW Certified Tech training (Level 3), a cabinet of exotic tools, a service lift, and a benevolent mentor to punch me in the back of the head every time I did something stupid. I seem to remember part of the operation even involving elevating the front wheel almost ninety degrees! But then, there it was, another diamond in the rough of assorted threads and posts: a link to a YouTube video on bleeding the rear brake fluid on an F-Twin!

Now, as we all know, how-to YouTube videos can be informative, hilarious, worthless, or even dangerous. My son-in-law, who was the one who prodded me into using forums and YouTube in the first place, tells me he particularly likes the home improvement videos that show the clips' producer/writer/actor suddenly pausing while fixing a sink valve or a three-way switch, saying something like "Huh, well, I've never seen that before." Again, just like typing, proficiency with a video camera and a laptop doesn't make anyone an impeccable source. I got lucky, though, and this clip on brake bleeding was thorough and easy to follow—the guy even had an acrobatic technique for simultaneously depressing the brake pedal (on the right side) and opening the bleeder valve (on the left) without an assistant! After assembling the needed tools and supplies (11mm wrench, torx set, .25" I.D. tubing, and DOT 4 fluid) and badgering my wife into working the brake, the operation only took fifteen minutes. And, in an unprecedented break with a long-standing tradition, I even avoided spilling stuff all over the driveway!

In my twenties, I had to face the fact that I was never going to be an NFL wide receiver or a Formula 1 driver, but I counted myself lucky I had at least emerged from the early seventies pretty much unscathed by civil unrest, war, and recreational drugs. As I slouch toward my seventies, I have to recognize that, much as I worship motorcycle mechanics, alas,

I'm never going to be one. However, thanks to the march of technology, I can count myself extremely lucky now to have access to the kind-hearted community of brothers and sisters just hovering out there in the ether, willing to help me with mechanical expertise, understanding, and support.

46
A PERFECTLY GOOD MOTORCYCLE

"Oh, it breaks my heart to see those stars

Smashing a perfectly good guitar,

I don't know who they think they are,

Smashing a perfectly good guitar"

When I first heard John Hiatt sing those lyrics, my thoughts went to the lead guitarist in the band I used to play with. For the ten years we were together, Steve never allowed anyone but himself to carry his guitars into or out of a gig. And immediately after the last encore, Steve could always be found sitting cross-legged back in a corner off stage, cradling in his lap the Telecaster, Strat, Gibson ES, or whatever six string he was having an affair with at the time. While the rest of us unplugged jacks, rolled cords, and schlepped equipment, Steve would be lovingly wiping his guitar down with polish and a pristine cloth diaper to remove the sweat and grime left from four hours of feeding a Marshall amp.

Hiatt's and my bandmate's revulsion at seeing a perfectly good guitar abused is the same way I felt watching an old CB360 weather the winter on its centerstand in a driveway I passed every day on the way to work. I eventually got the owner to sell it to me for a buck, but it was too far gone to resurrect, and I sadly gave it to a kid as a parts bike. I feel the same way now when I see a stunt rider balancing a bike on a front wheel or shooting off a steep motocross booter. Sure, those bikes might look spiffy, and like anyone, I'm awed by the skill, timing, and coordination of those riders, but for some reason, all I can think about are the poor, perfectly good motorcycles that probably got smashed during all the practices leading up to those performances.

I like looking at my motorcycle, at present, a shiny grey F 700 GS. Or maybe I should say I like the looks of the shiny grey, undamaged BMW. I shudder when I read about riders plowing their GSs into ravines filled with softball-sized rocks or skittering an S 1000 RR across the track, into the run-off area, and against the catch fence— shattered carbon fiber, gouged gas tanks, bent forks, oh my! And, years ago, when my bike and I slid sideways through an intersection dusted with flour-like sand, once out of danger, my first impulse was to check the bike over, rather than worry about my torn jeans and the landing strip of road rash strafed down my forearm.

This is why, once I could afford it (and Twisted Throttle conveniently put them on sale), I ordered a set of Givi crash bars. I told myself it was more than a farkle; it was insurance against broken directional stalks, cracked ABS plastic, bent levers, and grated engine cases. After one of my buddies got

T-boned by a driver running a stop sign, I took some comfort that the powder-coated cage might also provide a little more protection for my spindly legs.

Any reader of my columns is familiar with my meager wrenching skills; however, I thought with the proper instructions and some unaccustomed patience I could install the bars. I began by laying out all the parts, carefully writing their numbers with a Magic Marker on the concrete basement floor. (Once the parts were gone, it looked like a four-foot by four-foot connect-the-dots puzzle.) In a precedent-breaking act of heresy, I then begrudgingly consulted the sheet of sparse, wordless illustrations that passed for instructions.

For the next few hours, apart from keeping my Lab Penny out of my parts layout, everything went swimmingly...until I reached the final fastener. There was no mounting point on the frame for the last retaining bolt. Furious, I smoldered for a while, then shot off a blistering email rant to Twisted Throttle, dissembled the entire thing, and boxed it back up for return. With the last yard of packing tape applied and most of my exasperation spent, I had nagging second thoughts. Would Givi really make such a mistake? Could the problem possibly be . . . me?

Off came the packing tape and padding, and I went through the whole assembly once again, only to be stymied once more by the missing bolt hole. But wait; where is that rubber tube going? I plucked a little hose I later deduced was a breather out of the bolt hole meant for a crash bar mount, probably just stuck in there for shipping. Eureka! Suddenly everything came together! I had to make a sheepish apology to the Twisted Throttle tech and delete the ugly review I had posted (never touch a keyboard when you're angry), but he was quite understanding—probably not his first encounter with a mechanical moron like me.

As someone once told me, "There are riders who have dropped their bikes and riders who lie about it." If (when) I drop this F7, just like I've dropped every other bike I've had at one time or another, at least there's a good chance its looks will remain "perfectly good," and as an unexpected benefit, the whole crash bar experience gave me a more humble view of just who I think I am.

.

47

IN THE BEGINNING . . .

In Eau Claire, Wisconsin, where I've lived for the past year, there is a bar called Court'n House. It gets its name from the convenient escape hatch it offers from the county courthouse a block away. It's a pretty typical Wisconsin bar: a revolving list of twenty beers on tap, a tiny fry kitchen that cranks out hamburgers and one of the best Friday fish fries in town, and a standing room only crowd that swells to a raucous mob on Packer Sundays.

The last time I was there munching on a hamburger (two for one on Thursdays), I couldn't help overhearing snatches of conversation going on between two young women a stool or two down the bar. One of them used the word *motorcycle*, so naturally my ears perked up, and I zeroed in, while feigning absorption in a plate of fries and glass of Leinenkugel's . . .

"You're kidding, you're going to buy a motorcycle?"

"Yup, got the money, gonna buy it this winter. I've been watching a ton of videos, and I went to a cycle place last week."

"Like a Harley? Gonna get a leather jacket and a doo-rag?"

"No, not like that, something smaller. I think I'll ride it to work, and I want to ride in the woods, you know, on like, dirt trails. I mean, I'm not going to be jumping off hills and stuff, but maybe I'll ride to California this summer when I'm on vacation."

"Have you ever ridden one?"

"Well, no, but I found out there's a state class you can take in the spring; it's like a Saturday and Sunday, six or seven hours—they teach you everything."

I'm no expert on motorcycling (I might qualify as "seasoned"), but though that course she mentioned might earn her a license, I'm pretty sure it couldn't "teach you everything." This newbie motorcyclist might be naïve, but I found her wide-eyed optimism and self-confidence warmly endearing. It took me back.

Actually, compared to my introduction to riding, her approach sounded positively levelheaded. My first experience with bikes was a ride on the back on my older sister's boyfriend's Triumph when I was twelve. It was late one July evening, the air thick and soft in a blanket of humidity. I remember desperately clutching his sweaty white T-shirt (with the obligatory pack of Luckies rolled into one sleeve), as we ripped through town. But it had been enough. Back home, I watched my sister and her steady roar off, solemnly vowing to myself that I would have my own bike someday.

A few years later, a buddy down the street offered me his preposterously "customized" Honda S90 for fifty bucks (see "Little Bike, Big Lessons"), and with little to no experience with the interplay between clutches, shifters, and throttles, I bucked and stalled it home on the sidewalk in first gear.

For some reason, my dad had agreed to advance me the cash, possibly thinking the ridiculous bike posed little chance of ever taking me further than the end of the driveway. And when I got it home, he took on his usual bemused smirk over his son's pitiful excuse for intelligence. At that point, I suspect my parents felt their first three kids, spread over twelve years, had turned out pretty darned good, though they weren't exactly sure how that had happened, and eager to explore life as empty-nesters, they had basically adopted a *laissex-faire* policy when it came to rearing me. In fact, once I got my driver's license and joined a traveling band, I was more like a boarder than a family member in our big, nearly empty house. Sometimes I would disappear for days, playing gigs from one side of the state to the other, or I'd be busy running the fire lanes just outside town. Upon return, my mom might say, "You still live here?"

My parents' hands-off policy allowed me to wring out every bit of remaining life left in that poor Honda, and when I finally had enough of bump starting and certain insensitive remarks from my buddies, I boarded a long, twenty-year train of bike upgrades that eventually led me to a curious motorcycle dealership in tiny Hatley, Wisconsin, called S-K Service. The shop is as much a museum as a business, crammed with an eclectic mix of bikes ranging from one of the first Triumph Rocket IIIs to a Benelli that was sold through Montgomery Wards department stores. Nestled between a sexy Yamaha Radian and a pair of black Honda CB750s was an immaculately restored BMW R65. About all I knew about Beemers at the time was that the cylinders looked weird, but when I climbed aboard, well, it just felt right. Now, after another twenty more years and a progression of more and more recent BMWs, I'm a disciple.

How do people get sucked into this weird, solitary, and admittedly risky lifestyle? My pint glass empty and the bartender scribbling my bill, I leaned forward for a clue in the last few snatches of the bar stool conversation:

"But why do you want to ride a motorcycle?"

The young lady cocked her head and looked up at the soccer game playing on the screen above the bar, as if the answer might be there.

"I'm not sure, it's just something I dream of doing. I just want to ride."

More than words, her expression conveyed a familiar feeling. I couldn't help wishing she would get to live her dream.

Acknowledgements

Many thanks for their kind assistance and support to Mike Fitterling at Road Dog Publications, Bill Wiegand at *BMW Owners News*, Erica Janik at New Hampshire Public Radio, my faithful readers, my on again/off again riding buddy Ralph Barsema, and my more than understanding better half, Deb. Thanks also to Jerry Riederer for his help on "How to Lose Friends . . . " All images are original with the author.

Also from Road Dog Publications

Bonneville Go or Bust [1] [2] by Zoë Cano

A true story with a difference. Zoë had no experience for such a mammoth adventure of a lifetime but goes all out to make her dream come true to travel solo across the lesser known roads of the American continent on a classic motorcycle.

I loved reading this book. She has a way of putting you right into the scene. It was like riding on the back seat and experiencing this adventure along with Zoë.—★★★★ Amazon Review

Southern Escapades [1] [2] by Zoë Cano

As an encore to her cross country trip, Zoë rides along the tropical Gulf of Mexico and Atlantic Coast in Florida, through the forgotten back roads of Alabama and Georgia. This adventure uncovers the many hidden gems of lesser known places in these beautiful Southern states.

. . . Zoë has once again interested and entertained me with her American adventures. Her insightful prose is a delight to read and makes me want to visit the same places.—★★★★★ Amazon Review

Chilli, Skulls & Tequila [1] [2] by Zoë Cano

Zoe captures the spirit of beautiful Baja California, Mexico, with a solo 3,000 mile adventure encountering a myriad of surprises along the way and unique, out-of-the-way places tucked into Baja's forgotten corners.

Zoe adds hot chilli and spices to her stories, creating a truly mouth-watering reader's feast!—★★★★★ Waterstones Review

Hellbent for Paradise[1][2] *by Zoë Cano*
The inspiring—and often nail-biting—tale of Zoë's exploits roaming the jaw-dropping natural wonders of New Zealand on a mission to find her own paradise.

Motorcycles, Life, and . . . [1][2] *by Brent Allen*
Sit down at a table and talk motorcycles, life and . . . (fill in the blank) with award winning riding instructor and creator of the popular "Howzit Done?" video series, Brent "Capt. Crash" Allen. Here are his thoughts about riding and life and how they combine told in a lighthearted tone.

The Elemental Motorcyclist[1][2] *by Brent Allen*
Brent's second book offers more insights into life and riding and how they go together. This volume, while still told in the author's typical easy-going tone, gets down to more specifics about being a better rider.

A Short Ride in the Jungle[1][2] *by Antonia Bolingbroke-Kent*
A young woman tackles the famed Ho Chi Minh Trail alone on a diminutive pink Honda Cub armed only with her love of Southeast Asia, its people, and her wits.

Beads in the Headlight [1] *by Isabel Dyson*
A British couple tackle riding from Alaska to Tierra del Fuego two-up on a 31 year-old BMW "airhead." Join them on this epic journey across two continents.

A great blend of travel, motorcycling, determination, and humor.—★★★★★ Amazon Review

Chasing America [1][2] *by Tracy Farr*
Tracy Farr sets off on multiple legs of a motorcycle ride to the four corners of America in search of the essence of the land and its people.

In Search of Greener Grass [1] *by Graham Field*
With game show winnings and his KLR 650, Graham sets out solo for Mongolia & beyond. Foreword by Ted Simon

Eureka [1] by Graham Field

Graham sets out on a journey to Kazahkstan only to realize his contrived goal is not making him happy. He has a "Eureka!" moment, turns around, and begins to enjoy the ride as the ride itself becomes the destination.

Different Natures [1] by Graham Field

The story of two early journeys Graham made while living in the US, one north to Alaska and the other south through Mexico. Follow along as Graham tells the stories in his own unique way.

Thoughts on the Road [1] [2] by Michael Fitterling

The Editor of *Vintage Japanese Motorcycle Magazine* ponders his experiences with motorcycles and riding and how they've intersected and influenced his life.

Northeast by Northwest [1] [2] by Michael Fitterling

The author finds two motorcycle journeys of immense help staving off depression and the other effects of stress. Along the way, he discovers the beauty of North America and the kindness of its people.

> . . . *one of the most captivating stories I have read in a long time. Truly a MUST read!!*—★★★★★ Amazon Review

Hit the Road, Jac! [1] [2] by Jacqui Furneaux

At 50, Jacqui leaves her home and family, buys a motorcycle in India, and begins a seven-year world-wide journey with no particular plan. Along the way she comes to terms with herself and her family.

Asphalt & Dirt [1] [2] by Aaron Heinrich

A compilation of profiles of both famous figures in the motorcycle industry and relatively unknown people who ride, dispelling the myth of the stereotypical "biker" image.

A Tale of Two Dusters & Other Stories [1] [2] by Kirk Swanick

In this collection of tales, Kirk Swanick tells of growing up a gear-head behind both the wheels of muscle cars and the handlebars of motorcycles and describes the joys and trials of riding

Man in the Saddle[1][2] *by Paul van Hoof*
Aboard a 1975 Moto Guzzi V7, Paul starts out from Alaska for Ushuaia. Along the way there are many twists and turns, some which change his life forever. English translation from the original Dutch

The Wrong Way Round[1][2] *by Andy Benfield*
The tale of the first westerner to cross into Burma from India on a motorcycle in over fifty years. It's also the story of a man coming to grips with his age and his romance with a woman twelve years younger. The story unfolds along some of the world's most stunning landscapes as the couple hurtle toward Burma among the Himalayas.

Those Two Idiots![1][2] *by A. P. Atkinson*
Mayhem, mirth, and adventure follow two riders across two continents. Jack and Marcin set off for Thailand thinking they were prepared, more or less, but mostly less. This story if full of mishaps and triumphs told in an amusing self-deprecating style. Here is an honest overland excursion with all the highs and lows, wins and losses, wonderful people and low-lifes, and charms and pitfalls of the countries through which they travel.